Reading Comprehension and Skills: Grade 4

S0-BSO-756

Table of Contents

ISBN 978-1-60418-256-9
02-339111151

Ready-to-Use Ideas and Activities

This book was developed to help students master the basic skills necessary to become competent readers. The stronger their foundation in reading basics, the faster and easier students will be able to advance to more challenging texts.

Mastering the skills covered within the activity pages of this book is paramount for successful reading comprehension. The activities at the beginning of the book aim to build and reinforce vocabulary, the foundation of reading comprehension. These activities lead to practice with more advanced comprehension skills such as categorizing and using context to understand words. Then, at the end of the book, students begin to practice answering comprehension questions about progressively longer stories.

All students learn at their own rate; therefore, use your judgment to introduce concepts to students when developmentally appropriate.

Hands-On Learning

Hands-on learning reinforces the skills covered within the activity pages and improves students' potential for comprehension. One idea for a hands-on activity is to use the removable flash cards at the back of this book to play a game of bingo. To do this, make a copy of the bingo card (page 3) for each student. Write the flash card words on the board. Have students choose 24 of the words and write them in the empty spaces of their bingo cards in any order. When students have finished writing on their cards, gather the flash cards into a deck. Call out the words one at a time. Any student who has a word that you call out should make an *X* through the word on her card to cross it out. The student who crosses out five words in a row first (horizontally, vertically, or diagonally) wins the game by calling out, "Bingo!" To extend the game, continue playing until a student crosses out all of the words on his bingo card.

Comprehension Checks and Discussion

In addition to the activities in this book, support reading comprehension growth by reading stories in the classroom. After a story—or part of a story—is read, ask your students questions to ensure and enhance reading comprehension. The first type of question you might ask is a factual question. A factual question includes question words such as *who, what, when, where, how,* and *why.* For example, *How old is the character?, Where does the character live?, What time was it when. . .?,* or any other question that has a clear answer. You might also ask open-ended questions. These types of questions do not have a clear answer. They are based on opinions about the story, not on facts. For example, an open-ended question might be *Why do you think the character acted as he did?, How do you think the character felt about her actions or the actions of others?, What do you think the character will do next?,* or *What other ways could this story have ended?* As students learn to think about these questions as they read, they will retain more of the material and understand it at a higher level.

                                                                                       CD-104306 • © Carson-Dellosa

Vocabulary Bingo

		FREE		

Contractions

tion is two words that have been combined into one. The missing letters are represented by an apostrophe. Read the sentences below. Circle the correct contraction for the underlined word or words.

1. I <u>cannot</u> believe it is raining again today.

   couldn't   can't   could've

2. <u>You are</u> the smartest student in the class.

   You'll   You've   You're

3. You <u>should not</u> cross the street without looking both ways.

   should've   couldn't   shouldn't

4. That answer <u>does not</u> look correct to me.

   doesn't   don't   didn't

5. <u>That is</u> the best book I have ever read.

   That'll   That's   That'd

6. Mom and Dad say <u>we are</u> moving soon.

   we've   we'll   we're

7. They <u>are not</u> going with us to the movies.

   isn't   aren't   weren't

8. <u>It is</u> important to study before a test.

   Its   It'd   It's

9. <u>I have</u> learned a lot from my great-aunt.

   I've   I'm   I'll

10. This blouse <u>is not</u> my favorite one.

    aren't   haven't   isn't

Name _____

Contractions

A contraction is two words that have been combined into one. The missing letters are represented by an apostrophe. Read the sentences below. Circle the correct contraction for the underlined word or words.

1. I am going to my grandma's house after school.

    I've   I'm   I'll

2. We were not planning to go to the store, but we needed to buy milk.

    weren't   wasn't   where's

3. He is one of the baseball players.

    He's   He'll   He'd

4. I think they are wonderful people.

    they'll   they've   they're

5. He will not wear his glasses when he swims in the pool.

    wouldn't   would've   won't

6. I had not planned to study tonight, but I have homework.

    hadn't   hasn't   haven't

7. They are not in the same math class.

    aren't   weren't   isn't

8. She could not finish the race with a hurt foot.

    could've   can't   couldn't

9. It has not rained for over two months.

    hasn't   hadn't   haven't

10. She says she is going to Spain this summer.

    she'd   she's   she'll

Name _____

Contractions

A contraction is two words that have been combined into one. The missing letters are represented by an apostrophe. Read the sentences below. Circle the correct contraction for the underlined word or words.

1. <u>You have</u> done a great job on this project.

    You'll   You're   You've

2. My uncle says <u>he has</u> wanted to see that movie since it came out.

    he's   he'd   he'll

3. <u>You had</u> already left the party by the time she arrived.

    You'll   You're   You'd

4. My mom and stepdad say <u>they have</u> enjoyed my piano playing.

    they're   they've   they'll

5. It seems like <u>it has</u> been snowing for days.

    it'd   it'll   it's

6. The soccer players thought <u>they had</u> won the game.

    they'll   they'd   they're

7. My friends and I think <u>we have</u> solved the puzzle.

    we're   we'll   we've

8. <u>I would</u> rather read than ride my bicycle.

    I'd   I've   I'll

9. <u>I have</u> always wanted a little sister.

    I'll   I've   I'd

10. My teacher says <u>she has</u> finished grading our tests.

    she's   she'd   she'll

Name _____

Contractions

A contraction is two words that have been combined into one. The missing letters are represented by an apostrophe. Read the sentences below. Circle the correct contraction for the underlined word or words.

1. I have been trying to reach her all week.

    I'm   I'll   I've

2. The scientists think that they have finally found a cure.

    they've   they'll   they're

3. Our teacher says that we have won the school contest.

    we're   we've   we'll

4. Dad said we had made the right choice.

    we've   we'd   we'll

5. It has been a long, cold winter.

    It'll   It's   It'd

6. Sue says that she has sung in the choir for three years.

    she's   she'd   she'll

7. Tim and Delon thought that they had done a good job.

    they'd   they'll   they've

8. I had been home only a minute when the phone rang.

    I'm   I'd   I'll

9. We have finished all of our homework for the week.

    We're   We'll   We've

10. You have been my best friend since first grade.

    You'll   You're   You've

Contractions

A contraction is two words that have been combined into one. The missing letters are represented by an apostrophe. Read the sentences below. Circle the correct contraction for the underlined word or words.

1. <u>We will</u> go swimming again next summer.

   We've   We'll   We're

2. I think <u>I will</u> make an A on the next test.

   I've   I'm   I'll

3. Do you think <u>you will</u> enjoy the skit?

   you'll   you'd   you're

4. She <u>was not</u> the first person to finish the race.

   wasn't   won't   wouldn't

5. If the weather is bad tomorrow, <u>they will</u> stay home.

   they'd   they'll   they're

6. Patti believes <u>she will</u> be famous one day.

   she'll   she'd   she's

7. Mom says <u>it will</u> be winter before long.

   it'd   it's   it'll

8. <u>That will</u> be my last class of the day.

   That'd   That'll   That's

9. I <u>had not</u> finished reading the newspaper yet.

   hasn't   haven't   hadn't

10. He says <u>he will</u> finish raking the leaves this afternoon.

    he'd   he's   he'll

          CD-104306 • © Carson-Dellosa

Name _____

Prefixes: *un*

A prefix comes at the beginning of a word. The prefix *un* is used to make something into its opposite. Look at the words below. Write new words by adding *un* before each. Use the new words to fill in the blanks in the sentences below.

tangle   _____

usual   _____

happy   _____

limited   _____

common   _____

friendly   _____

certain   _____

able   _____

1. When I was walking to school this morning, I saw an _____ sight.

2. It is _____ to have snow here in October.

3. Her uncle was _____ whether he could attend the play.

4. If it is raining tomorrow, we will be _____ to run the relay.

5. At first, the girl seemed _____, but it turned out she was just shy.

6. We had _____ trips to the buffet during the all-you-can-eat lunch.

7. My teacher was _____ with the work I had turned in.

8. Maria finds it difficult to _____ her long hair.

Prefixes: *un*

A prefix comes at the beginning of a word. The prefix *un* is used to make something into its opposite. Look at the words below. Write new words by adding *un* before each. Use the new words to fill in the blanks in the sentences below.

tidy   _____

aware   _____

important   _____

safe   _____

lock   _____

like   _____

cover   _____

affected   _____

1. It can be _____ to ride your bicycle barefoot.

2. Kirby was _____ that the plan for the weekend had changed.

3. I used my key to _____ the door.

4. The parade was _____ by the dark clouds.

5. After I make my bed, I will _____ my pillow.

6. That painting is _____ any other I have seen.

7. Dad says it is _____ whether I am tall or short.

8. My brother's room was _____ before he cleaned it.

Name _____

Prefixes: *re*

A prefix comes at the beginning of a word. The prefix *re* means "to do something again." Look at the words below. Write new words by adding *re* before each. Use the new words to fill in the blanks in the sentences below.

fill   _____

build   _____

wire   _____

new   _____

read   _____

do   _____

appear   _____

write   _____

1. An electrician will _____ the fan to make it work.

2. After the teacher looks at our rough drafts, we will _____ our papers.

3. The flowers in the garden are gone, but they will _____ next spring.

4. I need to _____ my membership before it expires.

5. Jim had to _____ his poster after it got wet in the rain.

6. Dad will _____ the doghouse now that our puppy has grown.

7. I enjoyed the book so much that I am going to _____ it.

8. I asked Mom if I could _____ my drink.

Prefixes: *re*

A prefix comes at the beginning of a word. The prefix *re* means "to do something again." Look at the words below. Write new words by adding *re* before each. Use the new words to fill in the blanks in the sentences below.

view   _____

claim   _____

consider   _____

fuel   _____

turn   _____

tell   _____

wind   _____

cycle   _____

1. After school is out, I will _____ to my house for the day.

2. After speaking to her coach, Josie will _____ her decision to quit the team.

3. Mom stopped at the gas station to _____ her car on her way to work.

4. Our family tries to _____ products so that less trash goes into the landfill.

5. My neighbor came to _____ his lost dog.

6. Uncle Joe likes to _____ his favorite joke over and over again.

7. Mrs. Lu will _____ our science projects before the fair.

8. Please _____ the rope so that it does not get tangled.

Name _____

Prefixes: *under*

A prefix comes at the beginning of a word. The prefix *under* means "to be below another thing" or "to not have enough of something." Look at the words below. Use the new words to fill in the blanks in the sentences below.

stand   _____

taking   _____

ground   _____

cooked   _____

brush   _____

water   _____

foot   _____

cover   _____

1. The detective went _____ to solve the mystery.

2. This project is a large _____, but I know we can handle it.

3. The diver explored the _____ caves.

4. My dog always seems to be _____ when I am trying to walk.

5. Uncle Kieran thought the bread was ready to eat, but it was _____.

6. I _____ how to do the most difficult math problems.

7. Dad cleared away the _____ from our backyard.

8. Potatoes and peanuts both grow _____.

Prefixes: *after*

A prefix comes at the beginning of a word. The prefix *after* means "to come after or later than something." Look at the words below. Write new words by adding *after* before each. Use the new words to fill in the blanks in the sentences below.

noon   _____

effect   _____

taste   _____

school   _____

glow   _____

thought   _____

shock   _____

care   _____

1. After the operation, the nurses provided _____ to the patient.

2. The _____ of running the race was that I was tired the next day.

3. Mrs. Gwinn runs an _____ program for arts and crafts.

4. The _____ from the fireworks lit the sky for a moment.

5. After an earthquake, a city may have an _____.

6. Adding fresh strawberries was an _____, but they made the pancakes taste great!

7. The spicy food left a strong _____ in my mouth.

8. Every _____ I play with my friends down the street.

Name _____

Prefixes: *mis*

A prefix comes at the beginning of a word. The prefix *mis* means "to do something the wrong way." Look at the words below. Write new words by adding *mis* before each. Use the new words to fill in the blanks in the sentences below.

read   _____

matched   _____

labeled   _____

calculated   _____

addressed   _____

understood   _____

directed   _____

spelled   _____

1. My name was _____ in the newspaper article.

2. The books were _____ as science books instead of math.

3. I _____ the directions, so Mr. Estes explained them again.

4. The traffic was _____ to South Street instead of North Street.

5. I _____ the math problem when I worked it the first time.

6. He _____ the envelope with the wrong house number.

7. My socks were _____ because I got dressed too quickly.

8. Sara _____ the map and turned right instead of left.

Prefixes: *out*

A prefix comes at the beginning of a word. The prefix *out* means "to go beyond." Look at the words below. Write new words by adding *out* before each. Use the new words to fill in the blanks in the sentences below.

come _____

last _____

look _____

put _____

spoken _____

run _____

wit _____

numbered _____

1. Tina was able to _____ everyone else in the race.

2. The presidential candidates each had a different _____ on taxes.

3. Their team _____ ours by five people.

4. My aunt is quite _____ about her ideas on recycling.

5. I hope to _____ the other students during the spelling bee.

6. In the story, the clever hen was able to _____ the fox.

7. Jared was pleased with the _____ of his baseball game.

8. Our _____ has increased since we started working as a team.

Name _____

Prefixes: over

A prefix comes at the beginning of a word. The prefix over means "to go above or have too much of something." Look at the words below. Write new words by adding over before each. Use the new words to fill in the blanks in the sentences below.

see   _____

flow   _____

due   _____

night   _____

sight   _____

looked   _____

heat   _____

cast   _____

1. The bucket started to _____ after it had rained all week.

2. If you _____ the roast, it will be too dry.

3. My friends and I are planning an _____ slumber party.

4. When the clouds hid the sun, the sky was _____.

5. My library books will be _____ if I do not turn them in today.

6. The mistake in that book was an _____.

7. Miss Gomez _____ my name the first time she read the list.

8. Dad will _____ my brother's building project.

Prefixes: *be*

A prefix comes at the beginning of a word. The prefix *be* means "on or around" or "to cause something to happen." Look at the words below. Write new words by adding *be* before each. Use the new words to fill in the blanks in the sentences below.

fore _____

side _____

low _____

come _____

cause _____

ware _____

long _____

friend _____

1. I _____ to the science team and the art club.

2. Jamal said he liked the movie _____ it was funny.

3. If a new student comes to class, it is kind to _____ him.

4. The sign said to _____ of snakes on the trail.

5. There are roses growing _____ my bedroom window.

6. It is important to study _____ a test.

7. Cherie hopes to _____ an author one day.

8. Pattie sits _____ her best friend, Kara.

Name _____

Suffixes

A suffix comes at the end of a word. In the sentences below, choose the correct word for each blank.

beauty **beautiful**

1. The flower's _____ was rare. It was the most _____ flower in the whole field.

remark **remarkable**

2. Everyone thinks her talent is _____. People _____ on her skills every time they hear her sing.

intelligent **intelligence**

3. Albert Einstein was known for his great _____. He was said to be more _____ than most people.

vaccine **vaccination**

4. Jonas Salk developed a _____ for polio. Many children receive this _____ when they are young.

accident **accidental**

5. My involvement in the school play was _____. I signed the tryout list by _____.

assist **assistance**

6. We stopped to see if we could _____ the woman standing by her car. She thanked us for our _____.

happy **happiness**

7. I was very _____ to find my lost cat. My _____ was so great that I picked her up and gave her a hug.

graduate **graduation**

8. My cousin's high school _____ is next week. He will _____ at the top of his class.

Suffixes

A suffix comes at the end of a word. In the sentences below, choose the correct word for each blank.

admire   admiration

1. I have great _____ for my mother. Many other people _____ her too.

patience   patient

2. Juan is the most _____ person I know. He has _____ even with his little brothers.

management manage

3. Mrs. Han likes working in _____. She can _____ any project she tries.

inventor   invent

4. Thomas Edison was a great _____. He liked to _____ new things in his workshop.

hesitate   hesitation

5. Sometimes I _____ before making a decision. My _____ means that I am thinking about it.

brilliant   brilliance

6. The _____ of the light could be seen for miles. The light had a _____ glow.

frequency   frequent

7. I take _____ breaks when studying for a test. The _____ of my breaks decreases as I begin to understand the material better.

transmission   transmit

8. The radio station's _____ reaches for many miles. The station can _____ to several different cities.

Name _____

Suffixes

A suffix comes at the end of a word. In the sentences below, choose the correct word for each blank.

friend   **friendly**

1. My best _____ is Consuela. She is _____ to everyone.

teach   **teacher**

2. Steve would like to be a _____. He wants to _____ either social studies or art.

magnificence   **magnificent**

3. The painting was a _____ work of art. Its _____ was known throughout the world.

announcement   **announce**

4. The principal will make an important _____ this afternoon. She will _____ the winners of the school poster contest.

universe   **universal**

5. Earth is part of the vast _____. Gravity is a _____ scientific law.

astonishment   **astonish**

6. Shanika's piano playing will _____ the crowd. Their _____ will be great.

victory   **victorious**

7. Our soccer team was _____. Our coach led us to _____.

colonial   **colony**

8. Maryland is an original _____ of the United States. People in _____ times dressed differently than people do today.

Suffixes

A suffix comes at the end of a word. In the sentences below, choose the correct word for each blank.

behave   **behavior**

1. My puppy is learning to _____. Her _____ is very good.

approve   **approval**

2. We asked our teacher to _____ our project. She thought it was a great idea and gave us her _____.

fortunate   **fortune**

3. Raul could not believe his good _____. He thought he was _____ to be chosen as the lead in the class play.

organization   **organize**

4. My aunt is known for her _____. She can _____ even the most cluttered closet.

indicate   **indication**

5. Please _____ your interest in the club by signing the list. Your name is an _____ that you want to join.

similarity   **similar**

6. My sister and I do not look very _____. Our one _____ is that we both have blonde hair.

begin   **beginner**

7. Thomas will _____ trumpet lessons next year. He will be a _____ in the school band.

qualification   **qualify**

8. In order to _____ for a medal, you have to win this race. Your _____ is your ability to run fast.

CD-104306 • © Carson-Dellosa

Name _____

Suffixes

A suffix comes at the end of a word. In the sentences below, choose the correct word for each blank.

sleep   **sleepy**

1. Many people need eight hours of _____ a night. If they stay up too late, they are _____ the next day.

volcano   **volcanic**

2. We watched the news report about the _____ eruption. People living near the _____ had to vacate their homes.

electric   **electrician**

3. The _____ put a new light switch in our garage. She had to turn off the _____ supply first.

detective   **detect**

4. A _____ is someone who solves mysteries. He uses clues to _____ the answers.

compete   **competition**

5. Joella will _____ in the essay contest. I think she can win the _____.

value   **valuable**

6. Grandma's scrapbook is _____ to her. She says the _____ of her scrapbook is priceless.

activity   **active**

7. It is important to keep _____. Try to find an _____ you like.

gardener   **garden**

8. My aunt loves to work in the _____. She is a terrific _____ because her plants always grow tall.

Multiple Meanings

Many words have more than one meaning. Sometimes you can figure out the correct meaning by seeing how the word is used in a sentence. Read the sentences below. Circle the correct meaning for the underlined word in each sentence.

1. The sailor took the vessel out to sea.

   a. part of the body that moves blood   b. ship

2. The football player weaved through the other people on the field.

   a. moved in a zigzag manner   b. sewed cloth

3. The plot of the film was unusual.

   a. storyline   b. area of land

4. The beam from the powerful flashlight lit every corner.

   a. plank of wood   b. light

5. Please do not tread on the flowers.

   a. step heavily   b. part of a tire

6. The mayor proposed a new plan to control traffic.

   a. suggested   b. asked someone to marry

7. The glare from the sun hurt our eyes.

   a. frown   b. bright light

8. Larry was the sole winner of the spelling bee.

   a. part of the foot   b. only

Name _____

Multiple Meanings

Many words have more than one meaning. Sometimes you can figure out the correct meaning by seeing how the word is used in a sentence. Read the sentences below. Circle the correct meaning for the underlined word in each sentence.

1. She offered a concrete suggestion on how to create a plan.
   a. made of cement   b. solid

2. The large candle gave off a brilliant light.
   a. very smart   b. very bright

3. My goal is to become a famous scientist someday.
   a. ambition   b. points scored in some sports

4. The patch of pumpkins grew very well.
   a. area of land   b. scrap of cloth

5. When a storm is coming, my cat acts very odd.
   a. number that is not even   b. unusual

6. It is sometimes hard to be patient.
   a. calm about waiting   b. ill or injured person

7. It took several tries at walking before the baby felt stable on her feet.
   a. steady   b. place where horses are kept

8. All of his limbs were sore after he competed in the race.
   a. tree branches   b. arms and legs

Multiple Meanings

Many words have more than one meaning. Sometimes you can figure out the correct meaning by seeing how the word is used in a sentence. Read the sentences below. Circle the correct meaning for the underlined word in each sentence.

1. The principal idea in the essay is that recycling is important.

    a. school leader   b. main

2. Mom suggested I channel my energy into playing basketball.

    a. focus   b. body of water

3. The fish was covered in slimy scales.

    a. small, thin plates   b. instruments used for weighing

4. The *Titanic* began to sink after it hit an iceberg.

    a. place to put dishes   b. go underwater

5. I checked out a volume from the library.

    a. book   b. how loud something is

6. Stefan bought a bolt of cloth to make curtains.

    a. metal used to fasten   b. roll of fabric

7. Writing a thank-you note is a nice gesture.

    a. hand motion   b. idea

8. Eleanor's view is that riding a bike is fun.

    a. opinion   b. sight

Multiple Meanings

Many words have more than one meaning. Sometimes you can figure out the correct meaning by seeing how the word is used in a sentence. Read the sentences below. Circle the correct meaning for the underlined word in each sentence.

1. My stepdad says my mom is the <u>anchor</u> of our family.

   a. strong support   b. metal weight on a ship

2. The referee gave the <u>signal</u> to begin the game.

   a. motion   b. traffic light

3. Mom made sure the picture frame was <u>level</u> before hanging it on the wall.

   a. even on both sides   b. flat and smooth

4. As the tomatoes grew bigger, they began to <u>swell</u>.

   a. excellent   b. grow in size

5. Mrs. Chin used a baton to <u>conduct</u> the band.

   a. direct or guide   b. behave in a certain way

6. It took me a few hours to <u>recover</u> after the long hike.

   a. put new cloth over something   b. feel better

7. I wrote an <u>outline</u> before starting my essay.

   a. drawing around   b. list of important points

8. Milk will not <u>last</u> very long if you leave it outside in hot weather.

   a. remain fresh   b. the end of something

Multiple Meanings

Many words have more than one meaning. Sometimes you can figure out the correct meaning by seeing how the word is used in a sentence. Read the sentences below. Circle the correct meaning for the underlined word in each sentence.

1. We hailed a cab to go home after the play.

    a. ice from the sky   b. called for

2. The tone of the film was joyful.

    a. sound or vibration   b. mood

3. Do you know who coined the phrase "to each his own"?

    a. turned into money   b. made up

4. My brother hatched a plan to finish his homework and see the movie too.

    a. thought of   b. came out of an egg

5. Many members of royalty have titles like "emperor" or "queen."

    a. words that come before names   b. phrases that describe a book

6. We are having a major test on Friday that covers three chapters.

    a. person in the armed forces   b. important

7. Paulo was not present when the guest speaker came to school.

    a. gift   b. in attendance

8. Before my dog was trained, his behavior was too rough.

    a. rowdy or forceful   b. bumpy or jagged

Multiple Meanings

Many words have more than one meaning. Sometimes you can figure out the correct meaning by seeing how the word is used in a sentence. Read the sentences below. Circle the correct meaning for the underlined word in each sentence.

1. My aunt often works the night shift at her job.

   a. period of time

   b. to change or move

2. We stopped to pay a toll when we crossed the bridge.

   a. slight charge

   b. sound of a bell

3. The Olympic swimmer reached his peak during his best event.

   a. mountaintop

   b. best point of performance

4. Lan's pants had a trace of dirt on them.

   a. small mark

   b. to draw around something

5. Every time a truck goes by, it jars our living-room windows.

   a. pots

   b. rattles

6. I kept dwelling on my teacher's kind words after class.

   a. thinking about

   b. living place

7. Olivia thought she could spy a squirrel in the treetop.

   a. secret agent

   b. glimpse

8. A U.S. senator's term of office is six years.

   a. word or phrase

   b. length

Analogies

Analogies show relationships between words. For example, boy is to man as girl is to woman. The relationship between boy and man is the same as the relationship between girl and woman.

Find the missing word in each analogy below.

dinner	cool	poor	begin	down
small	toe	sad	walk	loud

1. Left is to right as up is to _____.

2. Hand is to finger as foot is to _____.

3. Dark is to light as breakfast is to _____.

4. Wide is to narrow as big is to _____.

5. Hot is to cold as warm is to _____.

6. Slow is to fast as happy is to _____.

7. Dim is to bright as rich is to _____.

8. Stay is to leave as run is to _____.

9. Shy is to outgoing as quiet is to _____.

10. Stop is to start as quit is to _____.

Analogies

Analogies show relationships between words. For example, boy is to man as girl is to woman. The relationship between boy and man is the same as the relationship between girl and woman.

Find the missing word in each analogy below.

year	puppy	healthy	wet	tale
lead	alert	yell	lower	messy

1. Pen is to ink as pencil is to _____.

2. Cat is to kitten as dog is to _____.

3. Asleep is to awake as tired is to _____.

4. Whisper is to shout as mumble is to _____.

5. Sick is to well as unhealthy is to _____.

6. Clean is to dirty as neat is to _____.

7. Old is to young as dry is to _____.

8. Fact is to fiction as article is to _____.

9. Open is to shut as raise is to _____.

10. Day is to week as month is to _____.

Analogies

Analogies show relationships between words. For example, boy is to man as girl is to woman. The relationship between boy and man is the same as the relationship between girl and woman.

Find the missing word in each analogy below.

flat	clear	relax	automobile	rectangle
foal	fabric	return	see	daybreak

1. Sunny is to overcast as foggy is to _____.

2. Rough is to smooth as bumpy is to _____.

3. Dusk is to nightfall as dawn is to _____.

4. Ship is to boat as car is to _____.

5. Scent is to smell as view is to _____.

6. Go is to stop as leave is to _____.

7. String is to thread as cloth is to _____.

8. Cow is to calf as horse is to _____.

9. Circle is to oval as square is to _____.

10. Work is to play as toil is to _____.

Analogies

Analogies show relationships between words. For example, boy is to man as girl is to woman. The relationship between boy and man is the same as the relationship between girl and woman.

Find the missing word in each analogy below.

shape	uncle	taste	road	summer
foot	eat	track	leaves	ape

1. Lion is to tiger as monkey is to _____.

2. Red is to color as triangle is to _____.

3. Cold is to winter as hot is to _____.

4. Eye is to see as tongue is to _____.

5. Mother is to father as aunt is to _____.

6. Glove is to hand as shoe is to _____.

7. Ship is to water as car is to _____.

8. Lemonade is to drink as sandwich is to _____.

9. Swimmer is to pool as runner is to _____.

10. Mow is to lawn as rake is to _____.

Analogies

Analogies show relationships between words. For example, <u>boy</u> is to <u>man</u> as <u>girl</u> is to <u>woman</u>. The relationship between <u>boy</u> and <u>man</u> is the same as the relationship between <u>girl</u> and <u>woman</u>.

Find the missing word in each analogy below.

shorts	dresser	hot	draw	stroll
sip	sentence	feathers	princess	orchestra

1. <u>King</u> is to <u>queen</u> as <u>prince</u> is to _____.

2. <u>Winter</u> is to <u>coat</u> as <u>summer</u> is to _____.

3. <u>Book</u> is to <u>chapter</u> as <u>paragraph</u> is to _____.

4. <u>Leap</u> is to <u>jump</u> as <u>walk</u> is to _____.

5. <u>Kitchen</u> is to <u>stove</u> as <u>bedroom</u> is to _____.

6. <u>Pen</u> is to <u>write</u> as <u>pencil</u> is to _____.

7. <u>Ice</u> is to <u>cold</u> as <u>soup</u> is to _____.

8. <u>Eat</u> is to <u>bite</u> as <u>drink</u> is to _____.

9. <u>Student</u> is to <u>class</u> as <u>musician</u> is to _____.

10. <u>Snake</u> is to <u>scales</u> as <u>bird</u> is to _____.

Compare and Contrast

Compare the words in each row below. Circle the two words that go together and write a sentence telling how the words are alike

1. exchange   return   reptile

_____

2. strange   bright   peculiar

_____

3. carnation   temperature   lily

_____

4. tablecloth   harmony   music

_____

5. blizzard   tornado   underground

_____

6. earnest   publish   sincere

_____

7. vessel   ship   suspend

_____

8. magnificent   encounter   marvelous

_____

Think About It!   **Choose one group and write a sentence using all three words.**

Compare and Contrast

Compare the words in each row below. Circle the two words that go together and write a sentence telling how the words are alike.

1. adapt   rotate   change

   _____

2. transmit   forecast   predict

   _____

3. voyage   suitcase   expedition

   _____

4. universal   widespread   Earth

   _____

5. stagger   retire   sway

   _____

6. scarce   thorough   careful

   _____

7. volcano   skyscraper   building

   _____

8. reveal   repair   uncover

   _____

Think About It! **Choose one group and write a sentence using all three words.**

Compare and Contrast

Compare the words in each row below. Circle the two words that go together and write a sentence telling how the words are alike.

1. acorn   oak   backyard

_____

2. edge   ceiling   boundary

_____

3. discard   maintain   keep

_____

4. horizon   sky   sailboat

_____

5. pebble   rock   ocean

_____

6. potato   sage   thyme

_____

7. genius   library   intelligence

_____

8. bronze   silver   ribbon

_____

Think About It!   **Choose one group and write a sentence using all three words.**

Compare and Contrast

Compare the words in each row below. Circle the two words that go together and write a sentence telling how the words are alike.

1. canyon   jeep   valley

_____

2. clothing   notebook   garment

_____

3. daily   never   frequent

_____

4. stroll   dash   gallop

_____

5. ankle   knee   helmet

_____

6. bison   piglet   buffalo

_____

7. thicket   grove   meadow

_____

8. scuff   polish   shine

_____

Think About It!   **Choose one group and write a sentence using all three words.**

Compare and Contrast

Compare the words in each row below. Circle the two words that go together and write a sentence telling how the words are alike.

1. weary   lively   tired

   _____

2. flag   zone   area

   _____

3. plunge   drop   climb

   _____

4. door   latch   lock

   _____

5. extend   close   reach

   _____

6. sad   lucky   fortunate

   _____

7. artificial   fake   natural

   _____

8. smooth   coarse   rough

   _____

Think About It! **Choose one group and write a sentence using all three words.**

Compare and Contrast

Compare the words in each row below. Circle the two words that go together and write a sentence telling how the words are alike.

1. professor   school   teacher

_____

2. grocery   quantity   amount

_____

3. twist   bend   straighten

_____

4. rescue   river   help

_____

5. grip   clasp   fingers

_____

6. apart   mingle   mix

_____

7. illustration   paragraph   drawing

_____

8. numerous   many   few

_____

Think About It! **Choose one group and write a sentence using all three words.**

Name _____

Read the story. Then, answer the questions.

What Are Symbols?

Symbols are things that stand for other things. We use symbols such as letters to stand for the sounds we make when we speak. The words made up by the letters stand for ideas. A symbol can tell how you feel about something. Your school might have a symbol such as a lion or a panther that stands for its teams. When you think of that animal, you feel pride in your school. Some symbols are used to stand for bigger things. The flag is a symbol of your country. A TV station might use a symbol to show the channel its programs are broadcast on. You can also see symbols in many buildings. Symbols help you know which restroom to use and which doors are accessible to people that use wheelchairs. These symbols are used as a kind of shorthand so that you can see the picture and quickly know what it means. Symbols are important in our everyday lives.

1. What is the main idea of this story?
    a. Symbols are important to our lives.
    b. Symbols can stand for animals.
    c. Symbols appear in many buildings.

2. What are symbols?

   _____

3. Where might you see a symbol?

   _____

4. Why might a school team use an animal as a symbol?

   _____

5. Why might a TV station use a symbol?

   _____

6. Why are symbols important?

   _____

   _____

Read the story. Then, answer the questions.

Country Flags

Each country of the world uses a different flag. The flag tells something special about that country. It may have colors that are important to that country's people. It may have a picture of an important animal. The flag of the United States has 13 stripes and 50 stars. The stripes represent the original 13 colonies, and the stars stand for the 50 states in the country today. The flag of Canada has a maple leaf. There are many maple trees in Canada. The red leaf is shown on a white band between two bands of red. The flag of Mexico also has three bands of color, but in the middle is a picture that represents the settling of Mexico. The picture shows an eagle holding a snake in its claws, sitting on top of a cactus. According to legend, the first settlers of Mexico saw this bird in the area where they would build their first city. This city is now the capital of Mexico.

1. What is the main idea of this story?
    a. The Canadian flag has red and white areas.
    b. The first settlers of Mexico saw an eagle.
    c. Flags tell something special about a country.

2. Why does each country have its own flag?

    _____

3. What things might you find on a flag?

    _____

4. What do the stripes and stars represent on the U.S. flag?

    _____

5. What does the maple leaf mean on the Canadian flag?

    _____

6. Describe the flag of Mexico.

    _____

    _____

    _____

Name _____

Read the story. Then, answer the questions.

Coats of Arms

A coat of arms is a special design used by a family or another group to show something special about that group. Coats of arms were used by knights in the Middle Ages to identify themselves. This design might be passed down through a family. A coat of arms often has an area called a "shield" in the middle. The shield may have different shapes or colors. Around the shield, there may be animals such as lions or eagles. Above the shield, there may be a special saying, such as "Knowledge and Honor." Countries sometimes use coats of arms as well. The Great Seal of the United States has many of the same elements as a coat of arms. It shows a bald eagle holding 13 arrows in one claw and an olive branch with 13 leaves in the other. The number of arrows and leaves stand for the 13 original states. The seal is used on important papers. It also appears on the U.S. one-dollar bill.

1. What is the main idea of this story?
   a. A coat of arms often has a shield on it.
   b. Coats of arms can stand for a family or another group.
   c. The Great Seal appears on the U.S. dollar bill.

2. What is a coat of arms?

   _____

   _____

3. How were coats of arms used in the Middle Ages?

   _____

4. What different things might appear on a shield?

   _____

5. What might appear above the shield?

   _____

6. Describe the Great Seal of the United States.

   _____

   _____

Read the story. Then, answer the questions.

Flowers to Remember

Many countries have special days to remember different people. These days have special flowers connected with them as well. Mother's Day is celebrated in Canada and the United States on the second Sunday in May. Many people give carnations to their mothers on Mother's Day. The flower for Grandparents' Day, which is celebrated on the first Sunday after the U.S. Labor Day, in September, is a forget-me-not. These flowers are small and blue and have a yellow center. Another special day is Veterans Day. On this U.S. holiday, people honor the soldiers who have served in the military. In Canada, this holiday is Remembrance Day, because people *remember* those who have served. Both of these holidays are observed on November 11 every year. In Canada, people wear poppies on their coats. Poppies are red flowers with a black middle. The flowers stand for the poppies that bloomed over a French battlefield during World War I.

1. What is the main idea of this story?
   a. Some people wear poppies on their coats.
   b. Different flowers are worn on special holidays.
   c. Special days help us remember different people.

2. When is Mother's Day celebrated in the United States and Canada?

   _____

3. What flowers are used for Mother's Day and Grandparents' Day?

   _____

4. What does *remembrance* mean?
   a. a type of poppy
   b. people who have served in the military
   c. remembering someone or something

5. When are Veterans Day and Remembrance Day celebrated?

   _____

6. What do the poppies worn on Remembrance Day stand for?

   _____

   _____

Name _____

Read the story. Then, answer the questions.

The Loon

The loon is the state bird of Minnesota (United States) and the provincial bird of Ontario (Canada). Loons can be found in the northern part of the United States and throughout most of Canada. A loon is about the size of a large duck and has a dark head and checkered gray and white feathers. Loons dive for fish in lakes as deep as about 200 feet (61 m) under the surface. They can swim for long distances underwater. Loons fly south to Mexico in the winter and come back north when the ice melts in the spring. In 1998, the Canadian postal service issued a special stamp worth one dollar that had a picture of a loon on it. The loon also appears on the Canadian dollar coin, which was introduced in 1987. This coin is often called the loonie. The Canadian two-dollar coin, introduced in 1996, features a polar bear. People call this coin the toonie.

1. What is the main idea of this story?
   a. Loons are special birds in Canada.
   b. Loons dive for fish underwater.
   c. The Canadian dollar coin is called the loonie.

2. Which U.S. state and Canadian province honor the loon?

   _____

3. Where are loons found?

   _____

   _____

4. What does a loon look like?

   _____

   _____

5. How was the loon recognized in 1998?

   _____

   _____

Read the story. Then, answer the questions.

Birthday Symbols

Many people recognize their birthdays by doing something special, such as inviting their friends over or having a family dinner. There are also special symbols that stand for the different months of the year, such as flowers and gemstones. Each of these also has a meaning connected with it. For example, the flower for March birthdays is the daffodil. This yellow flower represents happiness and friendship. The flower was chosen because it blooms during that month. Gemstones are another way of recognizing different birthday months. These pretty, sparkling rocks are polished and used to make jewelry. People might wear earrings, a necklace, or a pin with their birthstone in it. The gemstone for January is the deep red garnet stone. May's birthstone is an emerald, which is bright green. The most famous birthstone is probably the diamond, which stands for the month of April. On your next birthday, remember your special flower and gemstone too.

1. What is the main idea of this story?
    a. Stones and flowers always stand for the same thing.
    b. The daffodil is the flower for March.
    c. Each month has a special flower and stone.

2. What does the daffodil stand for?

    _____

3. How are birthday flowers chosen?

    _____

    _____

4. What are gemstones?
    a. polished rocks used in jewelry
    b. special kinds of flowers
    c. stones that are dull and gray

5. What do garnets and emeralds look like?

    _____

Read the story. Then, answer the questions.

Animal Symbols

Animals can mean different things to different people. To one family, a squirrel might be just a pest in the yard, but to another, a squirrel might serve as a reminder to put away food for the winter. A lion represents strength and courage, but it also stands for the country of Great Britain. It appears on the country's official coat of arms and reminds people of King Richard the Lionheart. The eagle stands for freedom, strength, and courage. It appears on the Great Seal of the United States and is also important in many American Indian cultures. Sports teams often choose an animal to represent them on the playing field. The team members remember their animal's qualities, such as speed and power, when they are playing. Some cars are also named after animals, such as a mustang or a ram, so that people will think the cars are as fast or as strong as those animals.

1. What is the main idea of this story?
   a. Animals are important symbols for different groups of people.
   b. Some cars are as fast as a mustang.
   c. Squirrels store food for the winter.

2. How might people see squirrels differently?

   _____

   _____

3. What does the lion stand for?

   _____

4. What does the eagle stand for?

   _____

5. Why might a sports team choose an animal to represent it?

   _____

   _____

6. Why are some cars named after animals?

   _____

Name _____

Read the story. Then, answer the questions.

Political Parties

Political parties are groups of people who feel the same way about one or more issues. Each party may work to elect several candidates to office, from the president down to the city mayor. Political parties often use symbols to represent them. When people see that symbol, they will think of the party. The donkey was first used in a political ad to represent President Andrew Jackson, who was a Democrat. Donkeys can be smart and courageous. The U.S. Republican Party symbol is the elephant. Elephants are known for their strength and intelligence. Both of these parties use red, white, and blue—the colors of the U.S. flag. Many of the Canadian political parties have maple leaves as part of their logos, or designs. The maple leaf appears on the Canadian flag, so this shows that the parties are tied to their country. Political parties in Great Britain use different symbols. The Labor Party uses the rose (the national flower), the Conservative Party uses the oak tree (for strength), and the Liberal Democrats use a dove (for peace).

1. What is the main idea of this story?
   a. Political parties work to elect people to office.
   b. Political parties use symbols to represent them.
   c. The Canadian flag has a maple leaf on it.

2. What are political parties?

   _____

   _____

3. Why does the Democratic Party use a donkey?

   _____

4. Why does the Republican Party use an elephant?

   _____

5. Why might a political party use symbols from its country's flag?

   _____

6. What are some symbols used by British political parties?

   _____

Name _____

Read the story. Then, answer the questions.

Symbols of Canadian Provinces

While Canada has many national symbols, such as the loon and the maple leaf, each of its provinces also has special symbols to represent it. Many of them have provincial plants, animals, and mottoes, or sayings. The province of Newfoundland and Labrador even has its own song! Alberta's official flower is the wild rose, and its bird is the great horned owl. Its motto is "strong and free," and its provincial fish is the bull trout. New Brunswick's flower is the purple violet. Its bird is the black-capped chickadee, and its tree is the balsam fir. Nova Scotia's official animal is a dog called the duck-tolling retriever. Its name means that it is good at finding ducks. Manitoba's bird is the great gray owl. Its official animal is the bison, and its tree is the white spruce. The province's motto is "glorious and free." Each province also has its own flag to show something about the history of that area.

1. What is the main idea of this story?
    a. Canadian provinces use symbols to tell something about them.
    b. Each province has its own flag.
    c. Canada has many national symbols.

2. What is a *motto*?
    a. an official flower
    b. a loon or a maple leaf
    c. a short saying that represents an idea

3. What is special about the province of Newfoundland and Labrador?

    _____

4. List the provincial flowers for two Canadian provinces.

    _____

5. List the provincial birds for two Canadian provinces.

    _____

6. What does a provincial flag tell you about that province?

    _____

Read the story. Then, answer the questions.

U.S. State Symbols

The United States has many national symbols that represent liberty and freedom. Each U.S. state also has its own symbols, including state animals, flowers, and flags. The state of Washington has a picture of George Washington, the first U.S. president, on its flag. The state fruit is the apple, and the state vegetable is the Walla Walla sweet onion, which grows in the city of Walla Walla. Louisiana has a pelican, the state bird, on its flag. The state reptile is the alligator. Alaska's flag shows a pattern of stars known as the Big Dipper. The state fish is the king salmon, and the state mineral is gold. Ohio's state insect is the ladybug. The state tree is the buckeye, and the state beverage is tomato juice. Texas is known as the Lone Star State because its flag has a single star on it. The state plant is the prickly pear cactus, and the state flower is the bluebonnet. Each state's symbols can tell you a lot about the plants and animals that live there.

1. What is the main idea of this story?
   a. National symbols represent liberty and freedom.
   b. U.S. states have many different symbols.
   c. The state tree of Ohio is the buckeye.

2. What are the state bird and reptile of Louisiana?

   _____

3. What does the Alaska flag look like?

   _____

4. Why is Texas called the Lone Star State?

   _____

5. What do a state's symbols tell you about it?

   _____

   _____

Name _____

Read the story. Then, answer the questions.

Smiley Face

You have probably seen a bright yellow smiley face in an ad or on a sign. Some people even wear them on T-shirts! The smiley face was created in 1963 by an artist named Harvey Ball. Ball was asked to come up with a symbol for an insurance company to use. The company wanted employees to feel cheerful about working for the company when they saw the smiley face. Ball drew something very simple and made the background yellow because it reminded him of the sun. Soon, the symbol became so popular that thousands of people outside the company were wearing smiley face buttons. In the 1970s, the smiley face was put on T-shirts, coffee mugs, and bumper stickers. It has brought a smile to many people's faces around the world. Today, people sometimes use smiley faces in their e-mails to represent different feelings. Harvey Ball probably never thought his symbol would still be used over 40 years later.

1. What is the main idea of this story?
   a. The smiley face is still used today.
   b. Harvey Ball created the smiley face.
   c. The smiley face is a simple symbol that has been around for a long time.

2. Why was the smiley face created?

   _____

   _____

3. Why did Harvey Ball make the background yellow?

   _____

4. How was the smiley face used in the 1970s?

   _____

5. How do people use the smiley face today?

   _____

   _____

6. Why is the smiley face so popular?

   _____

Read the story. Then, answer the questions.

Colors

Colors can symbolize different things. When you see the color orange, you might feel happy because it reminds you of a sunny day. It might make you feel warm. When you see the color blue, you might feel calm because it makes you think of a still lake. It might make you feel cool to think of swimming in the water. When you see the colors green, brown, and blue together, you might think of the beauty of nature. These colors are used on world globes. Colors can also be used to alert us to danger. Fire trucks are red so that people will notice them and move out of the way. Stoplights use colors to tell cars whether to move. A red light signals to stop, a green light signals to go, and a yellow light signals to yield, or to slow down and be more careful. Pay attention to the colors around you. They might help you in ways you do not expect.

1. What is the main idea of this story?
   a. Colors can mean many different things.
   b. A still lake might make you feel calm.
   c. Pay attention to the colors around you.

2. What does the color orange make you think of?

   _____

3. What does the color blue make you think of?

   _____

4. Why might green, brown, and blue make you think of nature?

   _____

5. Why are fire trucks red?

   _____

6. What do the colors on a stoplight mean?

   _____

   _____

Name _____

Read the story. Then, answer the questions.

Plant Parts

Plants have many parts. You can see some of them, and there are parts you cannot see. The plant begins with the root system underground. It sends out long, thin roots into the soil to gather water and minerals. The part of the plant that grows out of the ground is called the stem. The stem moves water and minerals from the soil up into the leaves. Sunlight helps the leaves make more food, which is moved to other parts of the plant. The leaves also produce the oxygen in the air we breathe. Some leaves have only one broad, flat area connected to the stem. Others have many leaflets, or slim, needle-like parts. Many plants have flowers at the top of the stem. The petals of a flower help attract bees and butterflies, which bring pollen from other flowers. The pollen helps the flower make new plants the next year. Some plants produce fruit. When the seeds in the middle of the fruit are planted, a new plant can grow.

1. What is the main idea of this story?
    a. A plant's root system is underground.
    b. Plants have parts such as roots, leaves, and petals.
    c. Bees and butterflies like flowers.

2. How does the root system help the plant?

    _____

3. What do leaves need to make food for the plant?

    _____

4. Describe two ways that leaves can look.

    _____

    _____

5. How do the petals of a flower help the plant?

    _____

6. What happens when seeds from fruit are planted?

    _____

Read the story. Then, answer the questions.

Ecosystems

All living plants and animals live in ecosystems. An ecosystem can be as large as Earth or as small as a puddle. A lizard might live in a desert ecosystem. A whale would live in an ocean ecosystem. In an ecosystem, all of the living things, such as plants and animals, and nonliving things, such as the soil and the weather, work together. Changing even one thing will affect the other parts of the ecosystem. For example, if the ecosystem where frogs live becomes polluted, the frogs may become sick. If something happens to the frogs, then the animals that eat them, such as snakes, will not have enough food. If there is a fire in a forest, then the mosses on the forest floor will not have shade to grow in. The ecosystem will change from one with large trees and plants that need cool temperatures to one with plants that do well with more sunlight. People must try to protect the ecosystems in which they live. It is important to remember that even if you cannot see every organism in the ecosystem, everything is connected.

1. What is the main idea of this story?
    a. In an ecosystem, everything is connected.
    b. Some ecosystems are forests, and some are deserts.
    c. Ecosystems can be large or small.

2. Name three types of ecosystems.

   _____

3. What happens if one thing is changed in an ecosystem?

   _____

4. What might happen if frogs in an ecosystem disappeared?

   _____

5. What might happen after a forest fire?

   _____

   _____

   _____

6. Why is it important to protect ecosystems?

   _____

Read the story. Then, answer the questions.

The Atmosphere

The atmosphere is the air that surrounds Earth. The air you breathe is part of the atmosphere. Earth's atmosphere contains the gases oxygen, nitrogen, and argon, along with dust, pollen, and water. Oxygen is the most important part of the atmosphere. It is made by plants during their food-making process. In addition to breathing the atmosphere, you can also feel it. When you feel a cool breeze in autumn or warm air on a summer day, you are feeling the atmosphere. The atmosphere has different layers. The troposphere is the layer above the surface of Earth. The troposphere makes up half the atmosphere. All weather occurs in this layer. The next layer is the stratosphere, where jets often fly. This layer absorbs much of the sun's harmful rays. In the mesosphere, the third layer of the atmosphere, rocks from space are caught and burned. The space shuttle orbits in the next layer, the thermosphere. The last layer is the exosphere. After that, you are out in space!

1. What is the main idea of this story?
   a. Air is made up of many gases.
   b. A cool breeze is part of the atmosphere.
   c. The atmosphere surrounds Earth and provides us with air.

2. What does Earth's atmosphere contain?

   _____

   _____

3. What are two ways you can feel the atmosphere?

   _____

4. List the layers of the atmosphere.

   _____

   _____

5. What important thing happens in the stratosphere?

   _____

6. In which layers of the atmosphere might you find man-made flying objects?

   _____

Read the story. Then, answer the questions.

Climate

The climate describes the weather in an area over a long period of time. If you live somewhere where there are large amounts of yearly rainfall, then you live in a rainy climate. If your town is very hot and dry, then you may live in a desert climate. Some cities, such as San Diego, California, have a very mild climate. Others, such as New Orleans, Louisiana, have warm, heavy air, so they have a humid climate. While the weather in a place may change from day to day, a region's climate seldom changes. Factors other than weather can also affect the climate in a given area. Areas that are close to the sea are cooler and wetter. They may also be cloudy, because clouds form when warm inland air meets the cooler air from the sea. Mountains may also affect climate. Because the temperature at the top of a mountain is cooler than at the ground level, the mountaintop may have year-round snow. Regions near Earth's middle, or equator, are warmer than those at the poles. Sunlight has farther to travel to get to the north and south poles, so these areas are much cooler.

1. What is the main idea of this story?
   a. Climate is the weather in a place over a long period of time.
   b. The north and south poles are very cold.
   c. Some climates are rainy, and some are very hot.

2. How are the climates of San Diego and New Orleans different?

   _____

3. What is the difference between weather and climate?

   _____

   _____

4. What climate might a city by the sea have?

   _____

5. What climate might be found on a mountain?

   _____

6. How are climates near the equator different from those at the poles?

   _____

Name _____

Read the story. Then, answer the questions.

Comets

Comets are objects that look like dirty snowballs flying through space. They have tails of dust that may be over 6 million miles (10 million km) long. Besides the tail, a comet has a nucleus, or center, made up of a closely packed ball of ice and dust. Surrounding the nucleus is a cloud of water and gases referred to as the coma. People can see comets only when they pass close to the sun. As they get closer to the sun, some of the ice in the nucleus melts, forming the long tail. Some comets appear after regular periods of time. Halley's Comet, named after Edmond Halley, the person who first predicted its return, passes through the solar system every 76 years. It was last seen in 1986 and will appear again in 2062. Earth is in no danger from comets. When the planet passes through the comet's tail, small pieces of rock called meteors fall into the atmosphere. Most of these are burned up in the mesosphere. They appear during a meteor shower as shooting stars.

1. What is the main idea of this story?
    a. Halley's Comet is very famous.
    b. Comets are objects from outer space made up of dust and ice.
    c. Comets are not dangerous to Earth.

2. Describe the parts of a comet.

    _____

    _____

3. What happens as a comet gets closer to the sun?

    _____

4. Who was Edmond Halley?

    _____

5. What is a meteor?
    a. a comet that passes by every 76 years
    b. ice from the comet's nucleus
    c. a small piece of rock from space

6. What happens when Earth passes through a comet's tail?

    _____

Name _____

Read the story. Then, answer the questions.

Vaccinations

Some people go to the doctor for shots called vaccinations. Vaccinations can protect people and animals from diseases. The first vaccination was developed by Edward Jenner, who was looking for a way to prevent smallpox in the late 1700s. Vaccinations work by injecting a dead or weak part of the disease into a person or animal. The body makes antibodies to fight the disease, and the person or animal then becomes immune to that disease. This means that they will not develop the disease, or they will have only a very mild form of it. The most important animal vaccine is for the disease rabies. Many cities require that people vaccinate their pets so that none of them will catch the disease from a wild animal. Some people build natural antibodies to the diseases in their area. If you visit another country, you may be required to get a vaccination for a disease that exists in that country. People who live there might have natural antibodies to the disease, but a visitor might not. Vaccinations can help build antibodies to diseases with which you would not normally come into contact.

1. What is the main idea of this story?
    a. Doctors give vaccinations.
    b. The first vaccination was developed by Edward Jenner.
    c. Vaccinations can help keep people and animals healthy.

2. What disease was the first vaccination developed to prevent?

    _____

3. How do vaccinations work?

    _____

    _____

4. What does it mean to become *immune* to something?
    a. to get a shot at the doctor's office
    b. to have little chance of getting sick from a disease
    c. to visit another country

5. Why might you need a vaccination when you visit another country?

    _____

    _____

 CD-104306 • © Carson-Dellosa

Read the story. Then, answer the questions.

Biofuels

Gasoline is used in cars, and oil is used to heat many homes. Biofuels have similar uses, but they are made from things like vegetable oil, which can be recycled and used again. Diesel is a type of fuel similar to heating oil. Diesel fuel is used in cars and trucks. Biodiesel, most of which is made from soybean oil, burns more cleanly than diesel. It can be used in diesel engines without having to add any special parts. Biodiesel produces less pollution, so it is better for the environment. Gasoline is known as a fossil fuel, which means that it comes from layers deep under the earth that are made up of plants and animals that lived millions of years ago. Biofuel comes from plants we grow today, so it is a renewable resource. Some biofuels are created from restaurants' leftover grease that was used to make foods such as french fries or fried chicken. Instead of throwing this grease away, people are finding ways to power their cars with it.

1. What is the main idea of this story?
    a. Biofuels are better for the environment than fossil fuels.
    b. Gasoline and diesel are used to power cars.
    c. Some people throw grease away after cooking.

2. What are biofuels?

_____

_____

3. Why might people choose to use biodiesel rather than diesel fuel?

_____

4. What is a fossil fuel?
    a. fuel used in cars and trucks
    b. grease used to make fried foods
    c. fuel made from plants and animals from long ago

5. What is a renewable resource?

_____

6. What are some things used to make biofuels?

_____

Name _____

Read the story. Then, answer the questions.

Endangered Species

Many species of animals around the world are endangered today. This means that there are very few of them left. Species sometimes become endangered through loss of habitat, as when a wilderness area is changed by building a city there. They may also become endangered when people hunt them for food or for their skin. Many countries keep lists of the species that live there and are endangered. People can work to protect these species' environments from further loss. They can also move animals to zoos or nature preserves to try to increase their numbers. When they think it is safe again, they will reintroduce the animal to its native habitat. The alligator was once on the U.S. Endangered Species List because many people liked to make shoes or purses from its tough hide. After a law was passed making it illegal to kill alligators, the number of alligators in the wild increased. In 1987, it was removed from the list. The alligator is an endangered species success story!

1. What is the main idea of this story?
   a. Many countries keep lists of endangered species.
   b. Areas can be changed when cities are built there.
   c. Many species of animals around the world are endangered.

2. What does it mean for an animal to be endangered?

   _____

3. How do species become endangered?

   _____

4. How do people work to protect species?

   _____

   _____

5. When do people take animals back to their native habitat?

   _____

6. Why was the alligator removed from the U.S. Endangered Species List?

   _____

   _____

 CD-104306 • © Carson-Dellosa

Name _____

Read the story. Then, answer the questions.

Volcanoes

Volcanoes are special mountains that sometimes shoot a hot liquid called lava into the air. Beneath a volcano is a pool of molten, or melted, rock. When the pressure underground builds up, the liquid is forced upward and out of the cone, or top, of the volcano. The liquid inside the volcano is called magma, but when it reaches the surface it is referred to as lava. A lava flow may travel down the sides of the volcano and over the land for several miles. As lava gets farther from the top of the volcano, it cools down and moves more slowly. Volcanic eruptions can be very harmful. Ash is sent into the air and can make it difficult to breathe. Rocks and lava from the eruption can flatten everything around the volcano, including forests and towns. Most volcanoes in the United States are located along the West Coast and in Hawaii and Alaska. The world's largest active volcano is in Mauna Loa, Hawaii. Another region of the world with many volcanoes is in the Pacific Ocean. This area is known as the Ring of Fire.

1. What is the main idea of this story?
   a. The Ring of Fire is located in the Pacific Ocean.
   b. Volcanoes shoot lava into the air and can be very dangerous.
   c. Lava flows can reach for miles around a volcano.

2. What is the *cone* of the volcano?
   a. the top, where lava shoots out
   b. the pool of molten rock underneath the earth
   c. the area around the volcano

3. What is the difference between magma and lava?

   _____

   _____

4. How can volcanoes be dangerous?

   _____

   _____

   _____

5. Where are most volcanoes in the United States located?

   _____

Read the story. Then, answer the questions.

Simple Machines

When you think of the word *machine*, you may picture a car engine or a lawnmower. These machines have many moving parts. Simple machines are tools that people use to make their work easier. They have very few parts. Instead of electric power, they use the energy of people to work. One simple machine is a lever. A lever is a board that rests on a turning point that makes it easier to lift things. A seesaw is a lever. Students on a seesaw use the board to make it easier to lift each other. Another simple machine is an inclined plane. To *incline* something means "to lean it against something else." An inclined plane is a flat surface that is higher on one end than the other. A ramp is an inclined plane. You might use a ramp to wheel a cart up to a curb instead of having to lift it. A slide is another inclined plane. Simple machines can make our lives easier in ways that are simple yet important.

1. What is the main idea of this story?
   a. Car engines and lawnmowers have many parts.
   b. A seesaw is a type of simple machine.
   c. Simple machines can make our lives much easier.

2. What do simple machines use instead of electricity?

   _____

3. What is a lever?

   _____

   _____

4. What does it mean to *incline*?
   a. lean at an angle
   b. use a simple machine
   c. play on a seesaw

5. What is an inclined plane?

   _____

6. What are two examples of simple machines?

   _____

Name _____

Read the story. Then, answer the questions.

Rainbows

You may have seen a rainbow in the sky after a rainstorm. A rainbow includes the colors red, orange, yellow, green, blue, indigo, and violet. You can remember the order of the colors with the name Roy G. Biv. All of the colors combined create white light. A rainbow is formed when a ray of sunlight shines through a cloud, refracts off the water droplets, and is split into bands of color. Rainbows are fairly rare to see. This is because special conditions are required for them to become visible. To see a rainbow, you must have rain in front of you, at a distance, and the sun behind you, low on the horizon. The curve of the rainbow is in the direction opposite from the sun. Rainbows are more common in summertime, because you must have both rain and warm sunlight to see them. Because there is less sunlight and more frozen water, rainbows are less likely to form during winter.

1. What is the main idea of this story?
   a. Rainbows are formed when light is split into bands.
   b. Rainbows are very rare.
   c. Rainbows have many colors in them.

2. What does Roy G. Biv stand for?

   _____

3. What do all the colors combined create?

   _____

4. How is a rainbow formed?

   _____

   _____

5. Why are rainbows rare to see?

   _____

   _____

6. Why are rainbows more common in the summertime?

   _____

e _____

Read the story. Then, answer the questions.

Atoms and Molecules

Everything around you is called matter—from your chair to your clothes to your family. Matter is made up of atoms and molecules, which are very tiny building blocks. Atoms make up chemical elements, such as the oxygen in the air you breathe. Atoms are combined to create molecules, such as the water you drink. Atoms are composed of even smaller particles called protons, neutrons, and electrons. A proton has a positive charge, an electron has a negative charge, and a neutron has no charge. The protons and neutrons stay together in the nucleus, or middle, while the electrons orbit, or move around, the atom. The number of protons determines the type of atom that is formed. Hydrogen is the simplest atom. It has only one proton. Oxygen has eight protons. Together, hydrogen and oxygen can form a molecule of water. Each water molecule has two hydrogen atoms and one oxygen atom. A glass of water contains too many molecules to count!

1. What is the main idea of this story?
   a. Atoms combine to make molecules.
   b. All matter is made up of atoms and molecules.
   c. A glass of water contains many molecules.

2. What are two examples of atoms?

   _____

3. What does *orbit* mean?
   a. stay in the middle
   b. a type of molecule
   c. move around something

4. Describe the differences between protons, neutrons, and electrons.

   _____

   _____

5. Why is hydrogen the simplest atom?

   _____

6. What is a water molecule made up of?

   _____

Name _____

Read the story. Then, answer the questions.

Bacteria

Your family or teachers may have told you to wash your hands with soap and hot water. This is to avoid the spread of bacteria. Bacteria are tiny organisms that live in your body and in the air, water, and soil. Bacteria are visible under a microscope. It would take one million bacteria to cover the head of a single pin! Bacteria may be small, but they can be very powerful. Some bacteria can cause infections such as a sore throat or cavities in your teeth. Not all bacteria are harmful, though. Your body has some good bacteria that help it digest food. Without bacteria, your intestines would not be able to gain the nutrition that they need from food and get rid of the waste that they do not need. Some bacteria are also used by scientists to make medicine and vaccines. In addition, they are used to make food such as cheese and yogurt. You should always wash your hands to ensure that you do not spread bad bacteria, but remember that some bacteria are good too.

1. What is the main idea of this story?
    a. Some bacteria are good, and some are bad.
    b. You should wash your hands before eating.
    c. Bacteria can be found in the air and the water.

2. Why should you wash your hands with soap and hot water?

    _____

3. What are two types of infections that bacteria can cause?

    _____

4. What do good bacteria in the body do?

    _____

    _____

5. How do scientists use bacteria?

    _____

6. What foods are bacteria used to make?

    _____

Name _____

Read the story. Then, answer the questions.

The Tundra

The tundra is a special type of land found in extremely cold areas such as the Arctic and parts of Alaska and Canada. The tundra is sometimes referred to as a frozen desert. In areas with tundra, the ground is frozen the whole year. This permanently frozen ground is called permafrost. Very short shrubs grow in the tundra. It is difficult for taller plants to grow because the ground is so cold and hard. The tundra can be very windy because there is so little to block the wind. Wind speeds can reach nearly 60 miles (about 100 kilometers) per hour. Few animals live in the tundra because there are not many plants. However, many birds and insects travel there in the summertime when the ice on the marshes and lakes melts. Because of the cold, windy conditions, it is difficult for people to live in areas with tundra. Some scientists work on research stations for part of the year to study the plants and animals that live there.

1. What is the main idea of this story?
   a. The tundra is very cold and windy.
   b. Some scientists live in the tundra.
   c. The tundra has difficult living conditions for animals and plants.

2. Where can the tundra be found?

   _____

   _____

3. What is permafrost?

   _____

4. Why is it hard for plants to grow in the tundra?

   _____

5. Why do birds and insects travel to the tundra in the summertime?

   _____

6. What do some scientists do in the tundra?

   _____

   _____

 CD-104306 • © Carson-Dellosa

Name _____

Read the story. Then, answer the questions.

Salmon

Animals such as dogs and cats may spend their entire lives in the same city or town in which they were born. Other animals, however, travel great distances during their life cycle. The salmon swims from the rivers of Alaska to the Pacific Ocean and back again. The salmon lays its eggs in the riverbed. After about three months, the eggs hatch. Then, the tiny fish swim around the rivers until they are large enough to travel to the sea. As the fish grow older and larger, they develop patterns that look like finger marks along their sides. Once they are one to three years old, they move in groups toward the ocean. Their bodies change so they can live in salt water instead of freshwater. The young salmon then spend several years swimming in the ocean. Eventually, they will swim back to the river in which they were born. There they lay eggs, and the cycle begins again.

1. What is the main idea of this story?
    a. Salmon travel great distances over their life cycle.
    b. Some animals may live in the same city their whole lives.
    c. Salmon lay eggs in streams or rivers.

2. Where do salmon travel during their life cycle?

    _____

3. How long does it take for salmon eggs to hatch?

    _____

4. How does the salmon's body change as it grows older?

    _____

    _____

    _____

5. What happens when the salmon are one to three years old?

    _____

6. Where does the salmon go to lay its eggs?

    _____

Read the story. Then, answer the questions.

The Aztecs

The Aztec people lived in the area that is now central Mexico. The Aztec Empire lasted from about 1325 to 1521 and stretched from the Pacific Ocean to the Gulf of Mexico. The Aztecs had a strong central government that was headed by a king or emperor. Under him were officials who governed different parts of the empire. The Aztecs enjoyed many foods, including corn or maize, beans, squash, tomatoes, and chili peppers. They sometimes added tomatoes and chili peppers. People in Mexico still eat many of these foods today. The Aztecs built temples that were similar to the Egyptian pyramids but without the pointed tops. On the outside of the temples were steps to the top, where there was a flat area. The Aztec people are known for their pottery and statues. They also made beautiful feathered headdresses, masks, shields, and clothing for their rulers to wear and use. You can find examples of Aztec crafts in museums today.

1. What is the main idea of this story?
    a. The Aztec people lived in the area that is now called Mexico.
    b. The Aztecs had a strong government and made many crafts.
    c. Aztec temples are like the Egyptian pyramids.

2. How long did the Aztec Empire last?

    _____

3. How was the Aztec government organized?

    _____

    _____

    _____

4. How are Aztec temples different from Egyptian pyramids?

    _____

    _____

5. What kinds of crafts did the Aztecs make?

    _____

    _____

Read the story. Then, answer the questions.

The Mississippi River

The Mississippi River is an important river for trade, recreation, and culture. It runs all the way from the U.S. state of Minnesota down to the Gulf of Mexico and covers 2,340 miles (3,770 km). The name *Mississippi* comes from an American Indian word meaning "great river." The first European explorer to reach the Mississippi was Hernando de Soto of Spain, who came there in 1541. In 1682 a group of French explorers claimed the river for their country. The city of New Orleans was built near the river in 1718. The United States acquired the area with the Louisiana Purchase of 1803. The Mississippi gained fame with the books of Mark Twain, which described life on the river. Twain, whose real name was Samuel Clemens, worked on a steamboat on the river in the late 1850s. Boats still travel down the Mississippi today, but people also water-ski and fish there. In addition, there are seven National Park Service areas along the river where people can go to enjoy nature.

1. What is the main idea of this story?
   a. The Mississippi River was made famous by Mark Twain.
   b. The Mississippi River was discovered by a Spanish explorer.
   c. The Mississippi River is important in many ways.

2. How long is the Mississippi?

   _____

3. Where did the Mississippi get its name?

   _____

4. Which countries' explorers visited the Mississippi?

   _____

5. Who was Samuel Clemens?

   _____

   _____

6. What do people do on and around the Mississippi today?

   _____

Read the story. Then, answer the questions.

Citizen Rights and Responsibilities

People who are citizens of a country have certain rights that belong to them. These rights are sometimes listed in the laws of that country. In Canada and the United States, citizens over the age of 18 are given the right to vote. Citizens also have the right to a fair trial and the right to speak freely about what they believe. They can practice any religion they want to, and they have the right to gather peacefully to exchange ideas. They have the right to ask their government to change laws that they think are wrong. With these rights come responsibilities too. People should obey the laws of their country. They should respect the opinions of others, even if they disagree with them. They should help others in their community and try to protect their environment. It is important to remember that all citizens are part of a large community and that everyone deserves to be treated fairly.

1. What is the main idea of this story?
    a. All citizens of a country have rights and responsibilities.
    b. Citizens have the right to vote.
    c. Everyone should be treated fairly in a community.

2. Where can you find a list of citizens' rights?

    _____

3. How old must citizens be to vote in Canada and the United States?

    _____

4. What are three rights in Canada and the United States?

    _____

    _____

5. What are three responsibilities in Canada and the United States?

    _____

    _____

6. Why is it important to treat all citizens fairly?

    _____

Read the story. Then, answer the questions.

Explorers of Canada

The first people known to have reached Canada from Europe were the Vikings, who sailed from Norway across the Atlantic Ocean around the year 1000. John Cabot traveled to Canada from Great Britain in the late 1490s. He was trying to reach Asia but instead found North America. Jacques Cartier sailed to Canada from France later in the 1500s and discovered the St. Lawrence River, which flows from the Atlantic Ocean to the Great Lakes. Samuel de Champlain came from France in the 1600s to explore the area that is now known as Quebec. He made 12 trips to the area he called New France, and he started the first permanent settlement at Quebec City. George Vancouver came from Great Britain in the late 1700s to explore North America. He mapped the entire western coastline, all the way from the Gulf of Mexico to southern Alaska! Both Vancouver Island and the city of Vancouver are named after him.

1. What is the main idea of this story?
   a. Sometimes areas are named after the people who explored them.
   b. The Vikings were the first to explore Canada.
   c. Many people have explored Canada throughout the ages.

2. What was John Cabot trying to do when he sailed to Canada?

   _____

3. What did Jacques Cartier discover?

   _____

4. Where was New France?

   _____

5. How was George Vancouver honored for his discoveries?

   _____

   _____

6. Which countries sent explorers to Canada or North America?

   _____

Read the story. Then, answer the questions.

Becoming a U.S. State

There are 50 states in the United States today. The last states to be added were Alaska and Hawaii, in 1959. Most states admitted to the Union after the original 13 were U.S. territories first. To become a state, the people of the territory had to band together with an organized government and then write a state constitution. After the U.S. Congress accepted the constitution, that territory became a state. Areas that might become U.S. states someday include the island of Puerto Rico and the District of Columbia. While people who live in these areas now are U.S. citizens, they have limited voting rights. Puerto Rico has a resident commissioner instead of a senator, and the District of Columbia has a non-voting member of the U.S. House of Representatives. Each of the 50 U.S. states has two senators and one or more representatives in Congress. Some people who live in areas of the United States that are not states believe they need a greater say in Congress. Others would like to keep their independence.

1. What is the main idea of this story?
    a. Becoming a U.S. state allows people living there to have a say in the national government.
    b. Puerto Rico and the District of Columbia are not states.
    c. Each state sends several people to Congress.

2. What were the last states to be added? When?

    _____

3. How does a U.S. territory become a state?

    _____

    _____

4. How are U.S. territories different from U.S. states?

    _____

    _____

5. How many members of Congress does each state have?

    _____

6. Why might someone living in a U.S. territory want statehood?

    _____

Name _____

Read the story. Then, answer the questions.

The Economy

You may have heard your family or a newscaster discuss the economy. The economy is a system in which goods and services are exchanged for money. Goods are things that are produced, such as books and clothing. Services are things people do for each other. For example, a teacher provides the service of educating students, and a police officer provides the service of keeping the community safe. Sometimes people provide a service that produces a good, such as a cook who prepares a meal that you can eat. People pay money for goods and services. When you give money to a producer of goods, she can purchase materials to make more goods. When you give money to a service provider, he may pay for more training to do his job better. They can also use the money to pay for basic items such as food and shelter. When newscasters report that the economy is strong, it means that most people are happy with the amount of money, goods, and services they have.

1. What is the main idea of this story?
    a. Newscasters often talk about the economy.
    b. Sometimes the economy is strong, and other times it is weak.
    c. The economy is a system in which goods and services are exchanged for money.

2. What are goods?

    _____

3. List two examples of goods.

    _____

4. What is a service?

    _____

5. List two examples of service providers.

    _____

6. What does it mean when newscasters say the economy is strong?

    _____

    _____

Read the story. Then, answer the questions.

World Holidays

People around the world celebrate different holidays. Both Canada and the United States have special days to mark the countries' birthdays. Canada Day is celebrated on July 1, and Independence Day in the United States is celebrated on July 4. On both of these holidays, people may have parades or picnics with their families. Many holidays have special foods associated with them. People may eat turkey on Thanksgiving or chocolate on Valentine's Day. During the Chinese Lantern Festival, people eat sticky rice dumplings. This holiday comes at the beginning of the Chinese New Year, in January or February, and has been celebrated for over 1,000 years! People in many other countries celebrate New Year's Eve on December 31. It is common for people to sing an old Scottish song called "Auld Lang Syne," which can be translated as "for old times' sake." They sing the song to remember the good times of the past and to look forward to more good times in the future.

1. What is the main idea of this story?
    a. Canada Day is celebrated on July 1.
    b. People around the world celebrate different holidays.
    c. Some people eat turkey at Thanksgiving.

2. How are Canada Day and Independence Day similar?

    _____

    _____

3. What are some foods eaten at holidays?

    _____

4. What festival is held at the Chinese New Year?

    _____

5. When is the Chinese New Year celebrated? When do other people celebrate the New Year?

    _____

6. Why do people sing "Auld Lang Syne"?

    _____

    _____

Name _____

Read the story. Then, answer the questions.

The Field Museum

The Field Museum is a famous museum in Chicago, Illinois. It contains exhibits of animals, plants, and people from around the world. The museum was built in 1893. It was first called the Columbian Museum of Chicago because it contained the objects for the World's Columbian Exposition of that year. Its name was changed in 1905 to honor Marshall Field, who was an early supporter. The Field Museum contains the skeleton of "Sue," the world's largest and most famous *Tyrannosaurus rex*. Visitors can find out what Sue ate and how she lived. The buildings around the museum include the Shedd Aquarium, which has marine life from tiny sea horses to large sharks, and the Adler Planetarium, where people can find out information about stars and planets. Museum workers conduct research on not only how animals have lived in the past, but how we can save endangered species today. People who visit the museum enjoy seeing the exhibits, but they also like finding out how they can help.

1. What is the main idea of this story?
   a. People like visiting the Field Museum.
   b. The Columbian Museum of Chicago was built in 1893.
   c. The Field Museum has exhibits on many animals, plants, and people.

2. Why was the name of the museum changed?

   _____

3. Who is "Sue"?

   _____

4. What can you see at the Shedd Aquarium?

   _____

5. What can you find out at the Adler Planetarium?

   _____

6. What are some things that museum workers do?

   _____

   _____

Read the story. Then, answer the questions.

City Services

Cities provide many services to people who live there. The mayor and city council, who are elected by the citizens of that city, make the laws that everyone must follow. They also meet to discuss community issues, such as whether to build a new recreation center. Other city employees include police officers and firefighters. These people work to keep everyone in the city safe. Other city services are at the library, where the public can check out books, and at companies that provide water and electricity. Some cities have special programs for the people who live there, such as reading clubs at the library or computer classes for senior citizens. It takes many services to make a city work. Some people like to give back to their community by doing volunteer work. They might teach swimming lessons or offer to pick up litter in the parks. When everyone in a city works together, it can be a great place to live.

1. What is the main idea of this story?
    a. People living in a city receive many services.
    b. Some people like to give back to their community.
    c. A library is a place where people can check out books.

2. Who elects the mayor and city council?

    _____

3. What do the mayor and city council members do?

    _____

    _____

4. Name three employees who work for the city.

    _____

5. What kinds of programs might a city have?

    _____

6. How can people help their community?

    _____

Read the story. Then, answer the questions.

Family Trees

Have you ever heard of a family tree? A family tree is not a plant that grows in the park. It is a drawing that shows how everyone in your family is related. The branches of the tree show different parts of your family. Before you begin to create a family tree, you should find out the names of as many family members as you can. Research this by asking your relatives. Then, begin to draw your tree. Write your name in the middle. Next to your name, write the names of your siblings. Above your name, write the names of your parents or stepparents. Above each of their names, write the names of their parents. You may want to draw a picture of each person or use photographs. Building the tree together can be a fun activity for the whole family. You may find out you are related to someone famous!

1. What is the main idea of this story?
   a. A family tree is not a plant that grows in the park.
   b. A family tree shows how everyone in your family is related.
   c. You may want to draw pictures on the family tree.

2. What do the branches of a family tree show?

   _____

3. Why should you talk to relatives about the family tree?

   _____

   _____

4. Where do you write your name on a family tree?

   _____

5. What goes above each name on a family tree?

   _____

6. What might you discover as you make your family tree?

   _____

Read the story. Then, answer the questions.

Reading Maps

Have you ever used a map to plan a route? A world map shows the outlines of the continents and seas. It may have parts shaded brown and green to show areas of desert or forest. A city map shows important buildings such as the library or city hall, as well as city streets. Maps use symbols to help you understand them. A compass rose looks like an eight-pointed star inside a circle. It shows you the directions north, south, east, and west. North is usually at the top. A map scale tells you how distances on the map relate to the real world. For example, one inch (2.5 cm) on the map may be equal to 100 miles (160.9 km). A map legend shows you what other symbols mean. A black dot may stand for a city, a star inside a circle may mean a country's capital city, and an airplane may be used to represent an airport. Knowing what these symbols mean makes it much easier to travel.

1. What is the main idea of this story?
   a. Some maps use a compass rose and a scale.
   b. A world map is very different from a city map.
   c. Maps use symbols to help you understand them.

2. What does a world map show you?

   _____

3. What does a city map show you?

   _____

4. Why do you use a compass rose?

   _____

5. What does a map scale tell you?

   _____

6. List some symbols used on a map.

   _____

Name _____

Latitude and Longitude

Read the story. Then, answer the questions.

Latitude and longitude are ways of dividing Earth into regions. Latitude lines run around the globe from east to west. The line around the middle is called the equator. Latitude is measured using the equator as zero. The lines around Earth as you move north are labeled with positive numbers. The lines going south are negative. Longitude lines run north to south from the north pole to the south pole. The zero point, called the Prime Meridian, for longitude is the line that runs through Greenwich, England. Positive values go east, and negative values go west. Both measurements are given in degrees. The latitude of Ottawa, the capital of Canada, is 45° 25′ 0″ N, which is read as "forty-five degrees, twenty-five minutes, zero seconds north." Latitude and longitude have long been used by people who study geography and map-making, as well as by explorers who travel around the globe. With the invention of the GPS, or global positioning system, many more people can find their exact location on Earth.

1. What is the main idea of this story?
   a. Latitude and longitude tell your exact location on Earth.
   b. Longitude is measured in degrees.
   c. The latitude of Ottawa is 45° 25′ 0″ N.

2. What is the line around the middle of Earth called?

   _____

3. Which places on Earth do longitude lines start and end at?

   _____

4. Where is the zero point for longitude?

   _____

5. Which people might use latitude and longitude most often?

   _____

   _____

6. Why might people want to know their exact location on Earth?

   _____

Nouns

A noun is a word that names a person, place, or thing. Read the story below. Some of the nouns are missing. Fill in the blanks with the words from the word box below.

bunch	dessert	table	grandmother	garden
backyard	cookbooks	dishes	pie	birthday
autumn	kitchen	recipes	flowers	house

Margie liked to visit her _____ after school. Grandmother's _____

was full of fun things to explore. In the _____ was a beautiful _____

with sweet-smelling _____. Margie had helped Grandmother plant them last

_____. Grandmother's large _____ had old _____ to

read through. They were filled with _____ for yummy _____. Margie's

favorite _____ was strawberry _____. She hoped Grandmother would

make one for her _____. Margie would offer to help! She would pick a

_____ of flowers for the dining room _____.

Nouns

A noun is a word that names a person, place, or thing. Read the story below. Some of the nouns are missing. Fill in the blanks with the words from the word box below.

apartment	brother	students	art	family
library	place	state	teacher	notice
school	work	mother	club	projects

Raven and her little _____ needed a new _____ to go after school.

They usually went to their aunt's _____, but she was moving to another

_____. Raven's _____ did not finish _____ early

enough to pick them up at school. Raven saw a _____ at _____ about

a new _____ that was forming. It was for _____ aged eight to ten. They

would meet after school, walk to the _____ with the art _____, and

work on art _____ until someone from their _____ could come get

them. Raven thought that was perfect! She loved _____, and so did her brother. She

could not wait to tell Mom.

Name _____

Cloze

Nouns

A noun is a word that names a person, place, or thing. Read the story below. Some of the nouns are missing. Fill in the blanks with the words from the word box below.

family	suit	hills	weekend	dad
neighborhood	park	socks	sister	store
hobby	morning	lunchtime	block	shoes

Lakshmi's _____ loved to run. He ran down the streets in their

_____ every _____ before sunrise. Then, he ran once around the

_____ at _____. He also ran up and down the steep

_____ by the city _____ each _____ morning. Lakshmi

thought this _____ looked like fun. She asked her dad if she could run with him. Dad

said, "Sure!" He took Lakshmi to the _____ to buy a track _____ and

_____ that would keep her feet dry. Finally, they bought running

_____. Now Lakshmi's older _____ wants to run too! Soon, her whole

_____ will be running.

82

CD-104306 • © Carson-Dellosa

Nouns

A noun is a word that names a person, place, or thing. Read the story below. Some of the nouns are missing. Fill in the blanks with the words from the word box below.

topic	something	class	model	magnets
salad	ideas	planets	system	tomatoes
advice	stepdad	project	plants	garden

Stefani needed to choose a creative _____ for science _____. First,

she wanted to study _____. She could show how to pull them apart. Then, she

thought she would build a _____ of the solar _____. She could show

how the different _____ moved. Finally, Stefani thought about growing tomato

_____. She liked working in the _____. Stefani had many good

_____. She asked her _____ which _____ to choose.

He said, "Pick _____ that the whole family will enjoy." Stefani thought that was great

_____. She decided to grow _____. She could make a tasty

_____ when she was done!

Verbs

A verb is a word that tells what kind of action is being performed. Read the story below. Some of the verbs are missing. Fill in the blanks with the words from the word box below.

hopes	practice	kicks	knows	move
quizzes	score	rides	runs	is
says	join	learn	tries	loves

Jamie _____ to be active. He _____ his bike after school, and he

_____ with his mom on weekends. He _____ to _____

the soccer team next year. His sister, Kim, has been helping him _____. She

_____ the goalie for the high school team. Jamie always _____ the ball

straight into the net when he plays with his sister. Kim _____ Jamie must

_____ all the rules before he _____ out for the team. She

_____ him on how to _____ a goal and when to _____

up the field. Kim _____ that Jamie will be a great addition to the team!

Verbs

A verb is a word that tells what kind of action is being performed. Read the story below. Some of the verbs are missing. Fill in the blanks with the words from the word box below.

fry	like	picks	tastes	stop
arrive	buy	helps	wait	take
have	wake	brings	puts	cast

Benny and his sister Hannah _____ to go fishing with their uncle. They

_____ up early on a Saturday morning. Uncle Ray _____ them up in his

old pickup truck. He _____ fishing rods and an icebox. They _____ to

_____ bait and cold drinks on the way to the lake. When they _____,

Uncle Ray _____ the bait on the hook. He _____ Benny and Hannah

_____ their lines into the water. Then, they _____ for a fish to

_____ the bait. Soon they _____ enough fish for dinner. They

_____ the fish with vegetables. It _____ great!

Verbs

A verb is a word that tells what kind of action is being performed. Read the story below. Some of the verbs are missing. Fill in the blanks with the words from the word box below.

laugh	watch	showed	dressed	sounded
went	were	felt	looked	smiled
play	loved	called	cheered	was

Keesha _____ to _____ her older sister, Kendra,

_____ volleyball. She _____ in the colors for Kendra's school and

_____ to all of the games. She _____ until she _____

hoarse. Kendra _____ Keesha her biggest fan. Keesha _____ sad that

she _____ too small to play volleyball. Kendra and the rest of her teammates

_____ very tall. One day Keesha's mom _____ her a picture of Kendra

when she was Keesha's age. Kendra _____ just like Keesha did now. Keesha

_____ and started to _____. "Kendra was small once too! Maybe I can

play volleyball one day after all."

Verbs

A verb is a word that tells what kind of action is being performed. Read the story below. Some of the verbs are missing. Fill in the blanks with the words from the word box below.

gets	called	has	walked	loves
started	come	exercise	stepped	would
does	walks	trusts	works	opened

Kamran _____ a new afterschool job. His neighbor, Mr. Quigley, just

_____ coaching soccer in the evenings, and he _____ not have time to

_____ home after work. Mr. Quigley said he _____ Kamran to

_____ his dog, Leo. Kamran _____ Leo to the park and back before he

_____ on his homework. On the first day of Kamran's new job, he

_____ the gate and _____ Leo's name. Leo came running. He was

ready for his walk! As Kamran and Leo _____ down the street, another neighbor, Mrs.

Pellini, _____ out of her house. She asked, "Kamran, _____ you walk

my dog too? Katie _____ to go to the park." Now Kamran _____ twice

the exercise!

Adjectives

An adjective is a word that describes something. Read the story below. Some of the adjectives are missing. Fill in the blanks with the words from the word box below.

enormous	beautiful	dark	quiet	awful
better	great	inspiring	fine	sad
nervous	cheerful	deep	bright	shaky

My choir director, Mrs. Rosas, is an _____ person. She helps us memorize

_____ songs so that we can give a _____ performance. When I tried

out for the choir, I was very _____. My voice was _____ and

_____, and I thought that I sounded _____. Mrs. Rosas smiled and said

she knew that I could do a _____ job. She told me to take a _____

breath and try the song again. This time I sounded _____! Our choir wears

_____ red shirts with _____ pants when we sing. Being in the choir

makes me feel _____. If I am _____ when I start singing, by the end of

the song I have an _____ smile on my face again.

CD-104306 • © Carson-Dellosa

Adjectives

An adjective is a word that describes something. Read the story below. Some of the adjectives are missing. Fill in the blanks with the words from the word box below.

marvelous	wonderful	older	fun	favorite
lengthy	yellow	giant	blue	nice
closest	fabulous	special	front	long

Leticia and her _____ brother, Amos, wanted to plan a _____

surprise party for their mom. She always threw parties for them that were _____ and

_____. Now it would be her own _____ day. Leticia made a

_____ list of all of her mom's _____ friends. Mom was such a

_____ person, everyone wanted to be her friend. Amos ordered a

_____ cake with _____ and _____ icing to feed all of

the guests. These were Mom's _____ colors. On the day of the party, Leticia asked

Mom to go on a _____ walk. When they got home, all of Mom's friends were hiding in

the living room. When Mom opened the _____ door, they all shouted, "Surprise!" Mom

said it was the most _____ party ever.

Name _____

Adjectives

An adjective is a word that describes something. Read the story below. Some of the adjectives are missing. Fill in the blanks with the words from the word box below.

famous	long	vast	slender	longer
brilliant	creative	green	deep	tall
dark	tiny	best	whole	great

Angelica decided to write a book. She loved to read, and her teachers said that she had a

_____ imagination. Her heroine would have _____ eyes and

_____, _____ hair, just like Angelica. She would live in the middle of a

_____, _____ forest. Angelica imagined the animals that might come

to visit her character— _____ bears, _____ deer, and

_____ mice. She worked on her story every day at lunchtime and after school. It grew

_____ and soon took up a _____ notebook! Angelica let her

_____ friend, Mindy, read her story. Mindy thought it was _____ and

very _____. She said she could not wait until Angelica was a _____

author one day!

Name _____

Adjectives

An adjective is a word that describes something. Read the story below. Some of the adjectives are missing. Fill in the blanks with the words from the word box below.

perfect	little	new	older	cute
thick	wide	bright	strong	old
entire	sturdy	soft	baby	yellow

Marcel's dad wanted to buy a _____ truck. His _____ one had too

_____ space for the _____ family to be comfortable. Marcel's mom

wanted something with _____ seats and room for his _____ sister's car

seat and her _____ dolls. Marcel's _____ brother wanted something

_____ enough to go camping in. Marcel thought it would be fun to have a

_____ yellow truck. His friends would love it! One day, Marcel's dad came home in a

new _____ truck. It had _____, _____ seats, and it was

_____ enough to go camping! Marcel thought it was the _____ truck

for their family.

Missing Words

Read the story below. Every tenth word is missing. Fill in the blanks with the words from the word box below.

the	did	They	needed
her	glad	Saturday	elderly
Amber	make	what	were

Amber belonged to a special club that met every _____. The club was not a sports team. The members _____ not play board games. It was a community club. _____ and her friends worked to make their neighborhood better. _____ made sure the sidewalks were clear and people's driveways _____ clean. They held yard sales to raise money to _____ new signs for the park so that people would know _____ time it closed. Amber's favorite project was helping the _____. She liked to help her grandmother, and many of _____ grandmother's friends lived in the same neighborhood. Sometimes they _____ their flowers watered or asked for help walking to _____ store. Helping others made Amber feel good. She was _____ she had joined the club!

Missing Words

Read the story below. Every tenth word is missing. Fill in the blanks with the words from the word box below.

gave	the	her	school
Bella	felt	along	their
out	Mabel	to	school

Bella and her classmates had been practicing for the _____ play for weeks. Bella

was playing the queen, and _____ friend Gerry was the king. They had made crowns

_____ of aluminum foil. Stacey and Aaron painted the posters _____

show the forest scene behind them. They would perform _____ play for all of the

younger students at their _____. Bella's little sister, Mabel, had been helping her

rehearse. _____ hoped Mabel would not try to say the lines _____ with

her! On the day of the play, Bella _____ nervous. She peeked out into the crowd and

saw _____ sitting with her friends. Mabel waved at her and _____ her

a smile. Bella began to relax. She knew _____ students would love the play.

Missing Words

Read the story below. Every eighth word is missing. Fill in the blanks with the words from the word box below.

He	let	play	giggle
small	dog	back	the
Warren	him	Warren	

Warren loved his new little puppy, Jojo. _____ had white fur and big brown eyes. _____ ran home from school every day to _____ Jojo out and play with him in _____ backyard. Jojo was always glad to see _____. Jojo licked Warren's hand and made him _____. Warren hoped he could teach Jojo to _____ fetch. His friend Vicky had a bigger _____ named Lucky. Lucky knew how to bring _____ sticks and tennis balls. Jojo was too _____ to carry a tennis ball now, but _____ knew he would grow bigger one day.

Name _____

Missing Words

Read the story below. Every eighth word is missing. Fill in the blanks with the words from the word box below.

keep	the	work	test
for	picnic	last	studied
news	the	to	proud

Julio had a wonderful surprise at school _____ week. He made the highest grade

in _____ class on his math test! Julio had _____ hard for a whole week

before the _____. He asked his stepmom to check over _____

problems he worked for practice. His hard _____ paid off! Julio ran home after school

_____ tell his dad and stepmom the good _____. They hugged him

and said they were _____ of him. They planned a special treat _____

the weekend. They went on a family _____ to the park. Julio thought he would

_____ working hard to do well in math.

Missing Words

Read the story below. Every fifth word is missing. Fill in the blanks with the words from the word box below.

their	Trudy	lived	dad
town	same	cousin	knew
Trudy	be	kept	good
and	family	had	but

Heidi and her cousin _____ were best friends. They _____ in different towns but _____ in touch by e-mail _____ telephone. One day Heidi's _____ said he had some _____ news for her. Trudy's _____ was moving to their _____! Heidi was excited. She _____ good friends at school, _____ they were not the _____ as having her own _____ in her class. She _____ her friends would like _____ too. And she would _____ a great addition to _____ soccer team!

Name _____

Missing Words

Read the story below. Every fifth word is missing. Fill in the blanks with the words from the word box below.

music	move	When	instrument
plays	Zak's	Now	is
a	his	him	it
Learning	claps	play	for

Zak is learning to _____ the violin. His stepdad _____

teaching him how to _____ the bow and place _____ fingers on

the strings. _____ Zak first started playing, _____ sounded like

fingernails on _____ chalkboard. His stepdad told _____ not

to give up. _____ to play a musical _____ takes time and patience.

_____ Zak can play melodies _____ his family. His stepdad

_____ along on the guitar. _____ little sister smiles

and _____ her hands to the _____.

Name _____

Point of View

Point of view refers to the person who is telling the story or "speaking." When you write a letter, you are writing in "first person," which includes the words *I, me, my, we,* and *our.* Second-person writing occurs when the author talks about *you* and *yours,* and third person includes the words *he, she, they, his, her,* and *their.* In third-person writing, the author does not put himself in the story.

A story can be told from different points of view.
In **first person**, the main character tells the story.
In **second person**, the story is told as though it is happening to you.
In **third person**, a narrator tells the story as if she is watching it happen.

Read each story and circle the point of view.

Marcus's family had just moved to a large city from a very small town. He was surprised at how many cars were on the street and how few people said hello when he met them on the sidewalk. In his old town, he had known everyone. He hoped that he would make a new friend on the first day of school. When he saw the crowded hallways as he walked into the building, he felt worried. Then, he thought to himself that with all those people around, he was sure to make a lot of friends.

First Person   **Second Person**   **Third Person**

When my family moved to the big city, I was excited about all of the new activities we could try. I never thought about how crowded it might be. Back home, my neighbors were very friendly. It seemed like I knew everyone in the whole town. I wanted to make new friends in the city, but when I got to school the hallways were so packed I could hardly get to my classroom. I took a deep breath and thought to myself, "With all of these people around, I am sure to make new friends."

First Person   **Second Person**   **Third Person**

You and your family have just moved to the city. You are surprised at seeing so many cars on the road. In your old town, you felt like you knew everyone. When you drive up to the school, your mother wishes you good luck. You walk into the building and start to look for your classroom. You think that with all these people around, you are sure to make some new friends.

First Person   **Second Person**   **Third Person**

Name _____

Point of View

Point of view refers to the person who is telling the story or "speaking." When you write a letter, you are writing in "first person," which includes the words *I, me, my, we,* and *our.* Second-person writing occurs when the author talks about *you* and *yours,* and third person includes the words *he, she, they, his, her,* and *their.* In third-person writing, the author does not put himself in the story.

A story can be told from different points of view.
In **first person**, the main character tells the story.
In **second person**, the story is told as though it is happening to you.
In **third person**, a narrator tells the story as if she is watching it happen.

Read each story and circle the point of view.

I love gardening. Seeing the little sprouts push up through the ground in early spring makes my heart sing. It can be hard to wait until the plants are fully grown to eat them. My brother likes vegetables, and he enjoys tomatoes in particular. Every year he tries to harvest them too early. At the end of the summer, I gather seeds and plant my crop for the next year. It is fun to see the whole growing cycle.

First Person   **Second Person**   **Third Person**

You love to work in the garden. You especially like seeing the tiny plants first appear through the dirt. Although it is hard to wait, you know that it is better to wait until the plants are fully grown before pulling them up. Your brother is so fond of tomatoes that his mouth begins to water even before they are red. At summer's end, you gather seeds to plant for next spring. You rejoice at the cycle of nature.

First Person   **Second Person**   **Third Person**

Carrie often worked in her garden. She checked the soil every morning to see if any new plants had appeared. Sometimes her brother tried to pick a green tomato, but she always stopped him. She said that it was better to wait until they were ripe. When the summer was over, she planted seeds for a new crop.

First Person   **Second Person**   **Third Person**

Name _____

Point of View

Point of view refers to the person who is telling the story or "speaking." When you write a letter, you are writing in "first person," which includes the words *I, me, my, we,* and *our.* Second-person writing occurs when the author talks about *you* and *yours,* and third person includes the words *he, she, they, his, her,* and *their.* In third-person writing, the author does not put himself in the story.

A story can be told from different points of view.

In **first person**, the main character tells the story.

In **second person**, the story is told as though it is happening to you.

In **third person**, a narrator tells the story as if she is watching it happen.

Read each story and circle the point of view.

Felipe loved to cook. He had been helping his mom and grandma in the kitchen ever since he could remember. One day Mom suggested he cook dinner for Grandma. Felipe was nervous but excited. He wrote a grocery list and asked Mom to take him shopping. They chose fresh vegetables and herbs for a delicious stew. Felipe had watched Grandma cook the stew many times. He thought he could cook it perfectly even without a recipe, as long as Mom was there to answer any questions.

First Person   **Second Person**   **Third Person**

I love to cook. I first started helping my mom and grandma in the kitchen when I was very small. One day Mom suggested I cook dinner for Grandma. I felt excited but also a little nervous. I had never cooked a meal by myself before! Mom and I went to the store with a list of food to buy. She showed me how to choose fresh vegetables and special herbs. I have watched Grandma make stew many times, so I think that I can cook it even without a list of instructions. Mom will be standing by to help just in case.

First Person   **Second Person**   **Third Person**

Your favorite activity is cooking. You have been helping your family in the kitchen since you were a child. One day your mom suggests you cook dinner for Grandma. You are excited but nervous, since you have never cooked a whole dinner by yourself before. You help your mom make a list of things to buy, and then you go to the store. You pick out only the freshest vegetables. Because you have watched Grandma make her special stew many times before, you know you can make it without using a recipe and with only a little help from Mom.

First Person   **Second Person**   **Third Person**

          CD-104306 • © Carson-Dellosa

Point of View

Point of view refers to the person who is telling the story or "speaking." When you write a letter, you are writing in "first person," which includes the words *I, me, my, we,* and *our.* Second-person writing occurs when the author talks about *you* and *yours,* and third person includes the words *he, she, they, his, her,* and *their.* In third-person writing, the author does not put himself in the story.

A story can be told from different points of view.
In **first person**, the main character tells the story.
In **second person**, the story is told as though it is happening to you.
In **third person**, a narrator tells the story as if she is watching it happen.

Read each story and circle the point of view.

You have been looking forward to the big class picnic for a long time. You and your friends hope to look for wildflowers after you eat lunch. You want to find 10 different kinds of flowers. When the day of the picnic comes, it starts to rain. You are sad at first, but then your teacher reminds you that the flowers need rain to grow. You smile to yourself and think that next time you can try to find 20 different wildflowers.

First Person   **Second Person**   **Third Person**

I had been looking forward to the class picnic for weeks. My friends and I were planning to pick wildflowers after eating our sandwiches. I hoped I could find 10 different kinds of flowers! On the day of the picnic, it was raining. I felt sad at first, but I knew that the rain would help the flowers grow even bigger. The next time we went on a picnic, maybe I could find 20 kinds of flowers!

First Person   **Second Person**   **Third Person**

Dreama and her friends had been looking forward to the class picnic all month long. They wanted to eat sandwiches in the field and then pick beautiful wildflowers. Dreama was hoping to find 10 different kinds of flowers. When she woke up on the day of the picnic, it was raining. Dreama felt sad at first, but she knew that the flowers needed rain to grow. Maybe at the next picnic she could find even more kinds of flowers.

First Person   **Second Person**   **Third Person**

Name _____

Point of View

Point of view refers to the person who is telling the story or "speaking." When you write a letter, you are writing in "first person," which includes the words *I, me, my, we,* and *our.* Second-person writing occurs when the author talks about *you* and *yours,* and third person includes the words *he, she, they, his, her,* and *their.* In third-person writing, the author does not put himself in the story.

A story can be told from different points of view.

In **first person**, the main character tells the story.

In **second person**, the story is told as though it is happening to you.

In **third person**, a narrator tells the story as if she is watching it happen.

Read each story and circle the point of view.

Clara ran home from school and checked the mailbox. She was disappointed to find that the mail had not come yet. She was expecting a letter from a special friend. Clara had a pen pal in Korea named Chi. They sometimes sent e-mail to each other, but both girls liked getting letters and funny postcards too. Just then there was a knock at the door. It was the postman! He smiled and handed Clara a letter with a Korean postmark.

First Person   **Second Person**   **Third Person**

I ran home from school yesterday and checked the mailbox. My letter from Chi was not there yet! Chi is my pen pal. She lives in Korea. We sometimes send e-mail to each other, but we both like getting postcards with funny pictures too. I was getting a snack when I heard a knock at the door. It was the mailman, and he had a letter for me! He smiled and said, "Tell Chi I said hello."

First Person   **Second Person**   **Third Person**

You run home from school to check the mailbox. You are disappointed when the letter you are expecting is not there. You are hoping for a letter from your pen pal, Chi, who lives in Korea. You like to send e-mail to each other, but you also like getting postcards and letters in the mail. You hear a knock at the door. It is the mailman, and he has a letter from Chi.

First Person   **Second Person**   **Third Person**

Point of View

Point of view refers to the person who is telling the story or "speaking." When you write a letter, you are writing in "first person," which includes the words *I, me, my, we,* and *our.* Second-person writing occurs when the author talks about *you* and *yours,* and third person includes the words *he, she, they, his, her,* and *their.* In third-person writing, the author does not put himself in the story.

A story can be told from different points of view.
In **first person**, the main character tells the story.
In **second person**, the story is told as though it is happening to you.
In **third person**, a narrator tells the story as if she is watching it happen.

Read each story and circle the point of view.

I like rain, and I like sun, but I like snow most of all. Winter is a fun season. I like building snowmen with my brothers and making a fort with snowballs. I like lying in the snow and making patterns with my arms. I help Dad shovel snow off the pathways so that people can walk and drive safely. I also help Mom make cocoa and cookies to warm us up when we come back indoors.

First Person   **Second Person**   **Third Person**

Lupe liked all kinds of weather, but she liked snow most of all. Winter was her favorite season. She liked to build snowmen with her brothers. Sometimes they made a fort with snowballs. Lupe liked to lie in the snow and make patterns with her arms. She helped her dad shovel the sidewalks so that people could walk safely. She also helped her mom make cocoa and bake cookies to warm everyone up when they came back indoors.

First Person   **Second Person**   **Third Person**

You like rain and sun, but you like the snow in winter most of all. You like to build snowmen with your brothers and make forts with snowballs. You like to lie in the snow and make patterns with your arms. You help your father move snow off the sidewalks. Then, you help your mom make cocoa and cookies to warm everyone up!

First Person   **Second Person**   **Third Person**

Worksheet — Page 4

Name _____ Decoding Contractions

Contractions

A contraction is two words that have been combined into one. The missing letters are represented by an apostrophe. Read the sentences below. Circle the correct contraction for the underlined word or words.

1. I cannot believe it is raining again today.
   couldn't (can't) could've

2. You are the smartest student in the class.
   You'll You've (You're)

3. You should not cross the street without looking both ways.
   should've couldn't (shouldn't)

4. That answer does not look correct to me.
   (doesn't) don't didn't

5. That is the best book I have ever read.
   That'll (That's) That'd

6. Mom and Dad say we are moving soon.
   we've we'll (we're)

7. They are not going with us to the movies.
   isn't (aren't) weren't

8. It is important to study before a test.
   Its It'd (It's)

9. I have learned a lot from my great-aunt.
   (I've) I'm I'll

10. This blouse is not my favorite one.
    aren't haven't (isn't)

CD-104306 • © Carson-Dellosa   4

Worksheet — Page 5

Name _____ Decoding Contractions

Contractions

A contraction is two words that have been combined into one. The missing letters are represented by an apostrophe. Read the sentences below. Circle the correct contraction for the underlined word or words.

1. I am going to my grandma's house after school.
   I've (I'm) I'll

2. We were not planning to go to the store, but we needed to buy milk.
   (weren't) wasn't where's

3. He is one of the baseball players.
   (He's) He'll He'd

4. I think they are wonderful people.
   they'll they've (they're)

5. He will not wear his glasses when he swims in the pool.
   wouldn't would've (won't)

6. I had not planned to study tonight, but I have homework.
   (hadn't) hasn't haven't

7. They are not in the same math class.
   (aren't) weren't isn't

8. She could not finish the race with a hurt foot.
   could've can't (couldn't)

9. It has not rained for over two months.
   (hasn't) hadn't haven't

10. She says she is going to Spain this summer.
    she'd (she's) she'll

CD-104306 • © Carson-Dellosa   5

Worksheet — Page 6

Name _____ Decoding Contractions

Contractions

A contraction is two words that have been combined into one. The missing letters are represented by an apostrophe. Read the sentences below. Circle the correct contraction for the underlined word or words.

1. You have done a great job on this project.
   You'll You're (You've)

2. My uncle says he has wanted to see that movie since it came out.
   (he's) he'd he'll

3. You had already left the party by the time she arrived.
   You'll You're (You'd)

4. My mom and stepdad say they have enjoyed my piano playing.
   they're (they've) they'll

5. It seems like it has been snowing for days.
   it'd it'll (it's)

6. The soccer players thought they had won the game.
   they'll (they'd) they're

7. My friends and I think we have solved the puzzle.
   we're we'll (we've)

8. I would rather read than ride my bicycle.
   (I'd) I've I'll

9. I have always wanted a little sister.
   I'll (I've) I'd

10. My teacher says she has finished grading our tests.
    (she's) she'd she'll

CD-104306 • © Carson-Dellosa   6

Worksheet — Page 7

Name _____ Decoding Contractions

Contractions

A contraction is two words that have been combined into one. The missing letters are represented by an apostrophe. Read the sentences below. Circle the correct contraction for the underlined word or words.

1. I have been trying to reach her all week.
   I'm I'll (I've)

2. The scientists think that they have finally found a cure.
   (they've) they'll they're

3. Our teacher says that we have won the school contest.
   we're (we've) we'll

4. Dad said we had made the right choice.
   we're (we'd) we'll

5. It has been a long, cold winter.
   It'll (It's) It'd

6. Sue says that she has sung in the choir for three years.
   (she's) she'd she'll

7. Tim and Delon thought that they had done a good job.
   (they'd) they'll they've

8. I had been home only a minute when the phone rang.
   I'm (I'd) I'll

9. We have finished all of our homework for the week.
   We're We'll (We've)

10. You have been my best friend since first grade.
    You'll You're (You've)

CD-104306 • © Carson-Dellosa   7

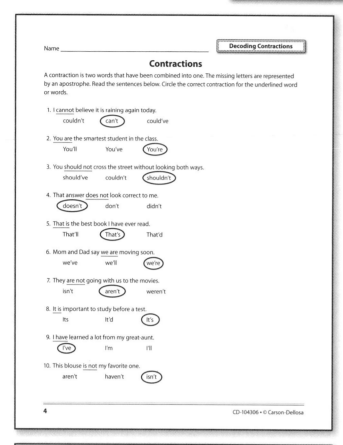

Worksheet 1 (page 8)

Name _____ **Decoding Contractions**

Contractions

A contraction is two words that have been combined into one. The missing letters are represented by an apostrophe. Read the sentences below. Circle the correct contraction for the underlined word or words.

1. We will go swimming again next summer.
We've (We'll) We're

2. I think I will make an A on the next test.
I've I'm (I'll)

3. Do you think you will enjoy the skit?
(you'll) you'd you're

4. She was not the first person to finish the race.
(wasn't) won't wouldn't

5. If the weather is bad tomorrow, they will stay home.
they'd (they'll) they're

6. Patti believes she will be famous one day.
(she'll) she'd she's

7. Mom says it will be winter before long.
it'd it's (it'll)

8. That will be my last class of the day.
That'd (That'll) That's

9. I had not finished reading the newspaper yet.
hasn't haven't (hadn't)

10. He says he will finish raking the leaves this afternoon.
he'd he's (he'll)

Worksheet 2 (page 9)

Name _____ **Prefixes**

Prefixes: un

A prefix comes at the beginning of a word. The prefix un is used to make something into its opposite. Look at the words below. Write new words by adding un before each. Use the new words to fill in the blanks in the sentences below.

tangle — untangle
usual — unusual
happy — unhappy
limited — unlimited
common — uncommon
friendly — unfriendly
certain — uncertain
able — unable

1. When I was walking to school this morning, I saw an **unusual** sight.
2. It is **uncommon** to have snow here in October.
3. Her uncle was **uncertain** whether he could attend the play.
4. If it is raining tomorrow, we will be **unable** to run the relay.
5. At first, the girl seemed **unfriendly**, but it turned out she was just shy.
6. We had **unlimited** trips to the buffet during the all-you-can-eat lunch.
7. My teacher was **unhappy** with the work I had turned in.
8. Maria finds it difficult to **untangle** her long hair.

Worksheet 3 (page 10)

Name _____ **Prefixes**

Prefixes: un

A prefix comes at the beginning of a word. The prefix un is used to make something into its opposite. Look at the words below. Write new words by adding un before each. Use the new words to fill in the blanks in the sentences below.

tidy — untidy
aware — unaware
important — unimportant
safe — unsafe
lock — unlock
like — unlike
cover — uncover
affected — unaffected

1. It can be **unsafe** to ride your bicycle barefoot.
2. Kirby was **unaware** that the plan for the weekend had changed.
3. I used my key to **unlock** the door.
4. The parade was **unaffected** by the dark clouds.
5. After I make my bed, I will **uncover** my pillow.
6. That painting is **unlike** any other I have seen.
7. Dad says it is **unimportant** whether I am tall or short.
8. My brother's room was **untidy** before he cleaned it.

Worksheet 4 (page 11)

Name _____ **Prefixes**

Prefixes: re

A prefix comes at the beginning of a word. The prefix re means "to do something again." Look at the words below. Write new words by adding re before each. Use the new words to fill in the blanks in the sentences below.

fill — refill
build — rebuild
wire — rewire
new — renew
read — reread
do — redo
appear — reappear
write — rewrite

1. An electrician will **rewire** the fan to make it work.
2. After the teacher looks at our rough drafts, we will **rewrite** our papers.
3. The flowers in the garden are gone, but they will **reappear** next spring.
4. I need to **renew** my membership before it expires.
5. Jim had to **redo** his poster after it got wet in the rain.
6. Dad will **rebuild** the doghouse now that our puppy has grown.
7. I enjoyed the book so much that I am going to **reread** it.
8. I asked Mom if I could **refill** my drink.

Name _____

Prefixes

Prefixes: *re*

A prefix comes at the beginning of a word. The prefix *re* means "to do something again." Look at the words below. Write new words by adding *re* before each. Use the new words to fill in the blanks in the sentences below.

view	review
claim	reclaim
consider	reconsider
fuel	refuel
turn	return
tell	retell
wind	rewind
cycle	recycle

1. After school is out, I will __return__ to my house for the day.
2. After speaking to her coach, Josie will __reconsider__ her decision to quit the team.
3. Mom stopped at the gas station to __refuel__ her car on her way to work.
4. Our family tries to __recycle__ products so that less trash goes into the landfill.
5. My neighbor came to __reclaim__ his lost dog.
6. Uncle Joe likes to __retell__ his favorite joke over and over again.
7. Mrs. Lu will __review__ our science projects before the fair.
8. Please __rewind__ the rope so that it does not get tangled.

Name _____

Prefixes

Prefixes: *under*

A prefix comes at the beginning of a word. The prefix *under* means "to be below another thing" or "to not have enough of something." Look at the words below. Use the new words to fill in the blanks in the sentences below.

stand	understand
taking	undertaking
ground	underground
cooked	undercooked
brush	underbrush
water	underwater
foot	underfoot
cover	undercover

1. The detective went __undercover__ to solve the mystery.
2. This project is a large __undertaking__, but I know we can handle it.
3. The diver explored the __underwater__ caves.
4. My dog always seems to be __underfoot__ when I am trying to walk.
5. Uncle Kieran thought the bread was ready to eat, but it was __undercooked__.
6. I __understand__ how to do the most difficult math problems.
7. Dad cleared away the __underbrush__ from our backyard.
8. Potatoes and peanuts both grow __underground__.

Name _____

Prefixes

Prefixes: *after*

A prefix comes at the beginning of a word. The prefix *after* means "to come after or later than something." Look at the words below. Write new words by adding *after* before each. Use the new words to fill in the blanks in the sentences below.

noon	afternoon
effect	aftereffect
taste	aftertaste
school	afterschool
glow	afterglow
thought	afterthought
shock	aftershock
care	aftercare

1. After the operation, the nurses provided __aftercare__ to the patient.
2. The __aftereffect__ of running the race was that I was tired the next day.
3. Mrs. Gwinn runs an __afterschool__ program for arts and crafts.
4. The __afterglow__ from the fireworks lit the sky for a moment.
5. After an earthquake, a city may have an __aftershock__.
6. Adding fresh strawberries was an __afterthought__, but they made the pancakes taste great!
7. The spicy food left a strong __aftertaste__ in my mouth.
8. Every __afternoon__ I play with my friends down the street.

Name _____

Prefixes

Prefixes: *mis*

A prefix comes at the beginning of a word. The prefix *mis* means "to do something the wrong way." Look at the words below. Write new words by adding *mis* before each. Use the new words to fill in the blanks in the sentences below.

read	misread
matched	mismatched
labeled	mislabeled
calculated	miscalculated
addressed	misaddressed
understood	misunderstood
directed	misdirected
spelled	misspelled

1. My name was __misspelled__ in the newspaper article.
2. The books were __mislabeled__ as science books instead of math.
3. I __misunderstood__ the directions, so Mr. Estes explained them again.
4. The traffic was __misdirected__ to South Street instead of North Street.
5. I __miscalculated__ the math problem when I worked it the first time.
6. He __misaddressed__ the envelope with the wrong house number.
7. My socks were __mismatched__ because I got dressed too quickly.
8. Sara __misread__ the map and turned right instead of left.

Name _____

Prefixes

Prefixes: *out*

A prefix comes at the beginning of a word. The prefix *out* means "to go beyond." Look at the words below. Write new words by adding *out* before each. Use the new words to fill in the blanks in the sentences below.

come	**outcome**
last	**outlast**
look	**outlook**
put	**output**
spoken	**outspoken**
run	**outrun**
wit	**outwit**
numbered	**outnumbered**

1. Tina was able to **outrun** everyone else in the race.
2. The presidential candidates each had a different **outlook** on taxes.
3. Their team **outnumbered** ours by five people.
4. My aunt is quite **outspoken** about her ideas on recycling.
5. I hope to **outlast** the other students during the spelling bee.
6. In the story, the clever hen was able to **outwit** the fox.
7. Jared was pleased with the **outcome** of his baseball game.
8. Our **output** has increased since we started working as a team.

16   CD-104306 • © Carson-Dellosa

Name _____

Prefixes

Prefixes: *over*

A prefix comes at the beginning of a word. The prefix *over* means "to go above or have too much of something." Look at the words below. Write new words by adding *over* before each. Use the new words to fill in the blanks in the sentences below.

see	**oversee**
flow	**overflow**
due	**overdue**
night	**overnight**
sight	**oversight**
looked	**overlooked**
heat	**overheat**
cast	**overcast**

1. The bucket started to **overflow** after it had rained all week.
2. If you **overheat** the roast, it will be too dry.
3. My friends and I are planning an **overnight** slumber party.
4. When the clouds hid the sun, the sky was **overcast**.
5. My library books will be **overdue** if I do not turn them in today.
6. The mistake in that book was an **oversight**.
7. Miss Gomez **overlooked** my name the first time she read the list.
8. Dad will **oversee** my brother's building project.

CD-104306 • © Carson-Dellosa   17

Name _____

Prefixes

Prefixes: *be*

A prefix comes at the beginning of a word. The prefix *be* means "on or around" or "to cause something to happen." Look at the words below. Write new words by adding *be* before each. Use the new words to fill in the blanks in the sentences below.

fore	**before**
side	**beside**
low	**below**
come	**become**
cause	**because**
ware	**beware**
long	**belong**
friend	**befriend**

1. I **belong** to the science team and the art club.
2. Jamal said he liked the movie **because** it was funny.
3. If a new student comes to class, it is kind to **befriend** him.
4. The sign said to **beware** of snakes on the trail.
5. There are roses growing **below** my bedroom window.
6. It is important to study **before** a test.
7. Cherie hopes to **become** an author one day.
8. Pattie sits **beside** her best friend, Kara.

18   CD-104306 • © Carson-Dellosa

Name _____

Suffixes

Suffixes

A suffix comes at the end of a word. In the sentences below, choose the correct word for each blank.

1.   beauty   beautiful
   The flower's **beauty** was rare. It was the most **beautiful** flower in the whole field.

2.   remark   remarkable
   Everyone thinks her talent is **remarkable**. People **remark** on her skills every time they hear her sing.

3.   intelligent   intelligence
   Albert Einstein was known for his great **intelligence**. He was said to be more **intelligent** than most people.

4.   vaccine   vaccination
   Jonas Salk developed a **vaccine** for polio. Many children receive this **vaccination** when they are young.

5.   accident   accidental
   My involvement in the school play was **accidental**. I signed the tryout list by **accident**.

6.   assist   assistance
   We stopped to see if we could **assist** the woman standing by her car. She thanked us for our **assistance**.

7.   happy   happiness
   I was very **happy** to find my lost cat. My **happiness** was so great that I picked her up and gave her a hug.

8.   graduate   graduation
   My cousin's high school **graduation** is next week. He will **graduate** at the top of his class.

CD-104306 • © Carson-Dellosa   19

Name _____

Suffixes

A suffix comes at the end of a word. In the sentences below, choose the correct word for each blank.

admire admiration

1. I have great **admiration** for my mother. Many other people **admire** her too.

patience patient

2. Juan is the most **patient** person I know. He has **patience** even with his little brothers.

management manage

3. Mrs. Han likes working in **management**. She can **manage** any project she tries.

inventor invent

4. Thomas Edison was a great **inventor**. He liked to **invent** new things in his workshop.

hesitate hesitation

5. Sometimes I **hesitate** before making a decision. My **hesitation** means that I am thinking about it.

brilliant brilliance

6. The **brilliance** of the light could be seen for miles. The light had a **brilliant** glow.

frequency frequent

7. I take **frequent** breaks when studying for a test. The **frequency** of my breaks decreases as I begin to understand the material better.

transmission transmit

8. The radio station's **transmission** reaches for many miles. The station can **transmit** to several different cities.

Name _____

Suffixes

A suffix comes at the end of a word. In the sentences below, choose the correct word for each blank.

friend friendly

1. My best **friend** is Consuela. She is **friendly** to everyone.

teach teacher

2. Steve would like to be a **teacher**. He wants to **teach** either social studies or art.

magnificence magnificent

3. The painting was a **magnificent** work of art. Its **magnificence** was known throughout the world.

announcement announce

4. The principal will make an important **announcement** this afternoon. She will **announce** the winners of the school poster contest.

universe universal

5. Earth is part of the vast **universe**. Gravity is a **universal** scientific law.

astonish astonish

6. Shanika's piano playing will **astonish** the crowd. Their **astonishment** will be great.

victory victorious

7. Our soccer team was **victorious**. Our coach led us to **victory**.

colonial colony

8. Maryland is an original **colony** of the United States. People in **colonial** times dressed differently than people do today.

Name _____

Suffixes

A suffix comes at the end of a word. In the sentences below, choose the correct word for each blank.

behave behavior

1. My puppy is learning to **behave**. Her **behavior** is very good.

approve approval

2. We asked our teacher to **approve** our project. She thought it was a great idea and gave us her **approval**.

fortunate fortune

3. Raul could not believe his good **fortune**. He thought he was **fortunate** to be chosen as the lead in the class play.

organization organize

4. My aunt is known for her **organization**. She can **organize** even the most cluttered closet.

indicate indication

5. Please **indicate** your interest in the club by signing the list. Your name is an **indication** that you want to join.

similarity similar

6. My sister and I do not look very **similar**. Our one **similarity** is that we both have blonde hair.

begin beginner

7. Thomas will **begin** trumpet lessons next year. He will be a **beginner** in the school band.

qualification qualify

8. In order to **qualify** for a medal, you have to win this race. Your **qualification** is your ability to run fast.

Name _____

Suffixes

A suffix comes at the end of a word. In the sentences below, choose the correct word for each blank.

sleep sleepy

1. Many people need eight hours of **sleep** a night. If they stay up too late, they are **sleepy** the next day.

volcano volcanic

2. We watched the news report about the **volcanic** eruption. People living near the **volcano** had to vacate their homes.

electric electrician

3. The **electrician** put a new light switch in our garage. She had to turn off the **electric** supply first.

detective detect

4. A **detective** is someone who solves mysteries. He uses clues to **detect** the answers.

compete competition

5. Joella will **compete** in the essay contest. I think she can win the **competition**.

value valuable

6. Grandma's scrapbook is **valuable** to her. She says the **value** of her scrapbook is priceless.

activity active

7. It is important to keep **active**. Try to find an **activity** you like.

gardener garden

8. My aunt loves to work in the **garden**. She is a terrific **gardener** because her plants always grow tall.

Vocabulary

Name _____

Multiple Meanings

Many words have more than one meaning. Sometimes you can figure out the correct meaning by seeing how the word is used in a sentence. Read the sentences below. Circle the correct meaning for the underlined word in each sentence.

1. The sailor took the vessel out to sea.
   a. part of the body that moves blood   (b.) ship

2. The football player weaved through the other people on the field.
   (a.) moved in a zigzag manner   b. sewed cloth

3. The plot of the film was unusual.
   (a.) storyline   b. area of land

4. The beam from the powerful flashlight lit every corner.
   a. plank of wood   (b.) light

5. Please do not tread on the flowers.
   (a.) step heavily   b. part of a tire

6. The mayor proposed a new plan to control traffic.
   (a.) suggested   b. asked someone to marry

7. The glare from the sun hurt our eyes.
   a. frown   (b.) bright light

8. Larry was the sole winner of the spelling bee.
   a. part of the foot   (b.) only

24   CD-104306 • © Carson-Dellosa

Name _____

Vocabulary

Multiple Meanings

Many words have more than one meaning. Sometimes you can figure out the correct meaning by seeing how the word is used in a sentence. Read the sentences below. Circle the correct meaning for the underlined word in each sentence.

1. She offered a concrete suggestion on how to create a plan.
   a. made of cement   (b.) solid

2. The large candle gave off a brilliant light.
   a. very smart   (b.) very bright

3. My goal is to become a famous scientist someday.
   (a.) ambition   b. points scored in some sports

4. The patch of pumpkins grew very well.
   (a.) area of land   b. scrap of cloth

5. When a storm is coming, my cat acts very odd.
   a. number that is not even   (b.) unusual

6. It is sometimes hard to be patient.
   (a.) calm about waiting   b. ill or injured person

7. It took several tries at walking before the baby felt stable on her feet.
   (a.) steady   b. place where horses are kept

8. All of his limbs were sore after he competed in the race.
   a. tree branches   (b.) arms and legs

CD-104306 • © Carson-Dellosa   25

Name _____

Vocabulary

Multiple Meanings

Many words have more than one meaning. Sometimes you can figure out the correct meaning by seeing how the word is used in a sentence. Read the sentences below. Circle the correct meaning for the underlined word in each sentence.

1. The principal idea in the essay is that recycling is important.
   a. school leader   (b.) main

2. Mom suggested I channel my energy into playing basketball.
   (a.) focus   b. body of water

3. The fish was covered in slimy scales.
   (a.) small, thin plates   b. instruments used for weighing

4. The Titanic began to sink after it hit an iceberg.
   a. place to put dishes   (b.) go underwater

5. I checked out a volume from the library.
   (a.) book   b. how loud something is

6. Stefan bought a bolt of cloth to make curtains.
   a. metal used to fasten   (b.) roll of fabric

7. Writing a thank-you note is a nice gesture.
   a. hand motion   (b.) idea

8. Eleanor's view is that riding a bike is fun.
   (a.) opinion   b. sight

26   CD-104306 • © Carson-Dellosa

Name _____

Vocabulary

Multiple Meanings

Many words have more than one meaning. Sometimes you can figure out the correct meaning by seeing how the word is used in a sentence. Read the sentences below. Circle the correct meaning for the underlined word in each sentence.

1. My stepdad says my mom is the anchor of our family.
   (a.) strong support   b. metal weight on a ship

2. The referee gave the signal to begin the game.
   (a.) motion   b. traffic light

3. Mom made sure the picture frame was level before hanging it on the wall.
   (a.) even on both sides   b. flat and smooth

4. As the tomatoes grew bigger, they began to swell.
   a. excellent   (b.) grow in size

5. Mrs. Chin used a baton to conduct the band.
   (a.) direct or guide   b. behave in a certain way

6. It took me a few hours to recover after the long hike.
   a. put new cloth over something   (b.) feel better

7. I wrote an outline before starting my essay.
   a. drawing around   (b.) list of important points

8. Milk will not last very long if you leave it outside in hot weather.
   (a.) remain fresh   b. the end of something

CD-104306 • © Carson-Dellosa   27

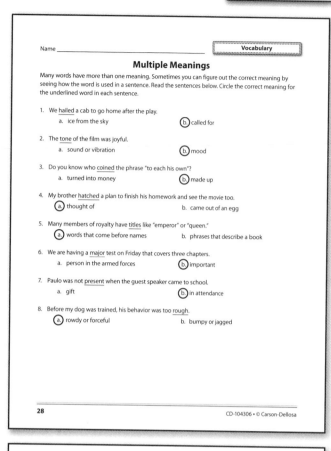

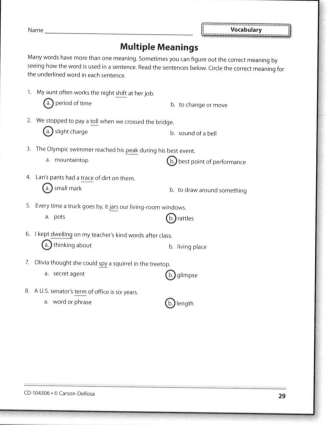

Name _____   Vocabulary

Multiple Meanings

Many words have more than one meaning. Sometimes you can figure out the correct meaning by seeing how the word is used in a sentence. Read the sentences below. Circle the correct meaning for the underlined word in each sentence.

1. We hailed a cab to go home after the play.
   a. ice from the sky   **b.** called for

2. The tone of the film was joyful.
   a. sound or vibration   **b.** mood

3. Do you know who coined the phrase "to each his own"?
   a. turned into money   **b.** made up

4. My brother hatched a plan to finish his homework and see the movie too.
   a. thought of   b. came out of an egg

5. Many members of royalty have titles like "emperor" or "queen."
   a. words that come before names   b. phrases that describe a book

6. We are having a major test on Friday that covers three chapters.
   a. person in the armed forces   **b.** important

7. Paulo was not present when the guest speaker came to school.
   a. gift   **b.** in attendance

8. Before my dog was trained, his behavior was too rough.
   a. rowdy or forceful   b. bumpy or jagged

Name _____   Vocabulary

Multiple Meanings

Many words have more than one meaning. Sometimes you can figure out the correct meaning by seeing how the word is used in a sentence. Read the sentences below. Circle the correct meaning for the underlined word in each sentence.

1. My aunt often works the night shift at her job.
   a. period of time   b. to change or move

2. We stopped to pay a toll when we crossed the bridge.
   a. slight charge   b. sound of a bell

3. The Olympic swimmer reached his peak during his best event.
   a. mountaintop   **b.** best point of performance

4. Lan's pants had a trace of dirt on them.
   a. small mark   b. to draw around something

5. Every time a truck goes by, it jars our living-room windows.
   a. pots   **b.** rattles

6. I kept dwelling on my teacher's kind words after class.
   a. thinking about   b. living place

7. Olivia thought she could spy a squirrel in the treetop.
   a. secret agent   **b.** glimpse

8. A U.S. senator's term of office is six years.
   a. word or phrase   **b.** length

Name _____   Vocabulary

Analogies

Analogies show relationships between words. For example, boy is to man as girl is to woman. The relationship between boy and man is the same as the relationship between girl and woman.

Find the missing word in each analogy below.

| dinner | cool | poor | begin | down |
| small | toe | sad | walk | loud |

1. Left is to right as up is to **down**.
2. Hand is to finger as foot is to **toe**.
3. Dark is to light as breakfast is to **dinner**.
4. Wide is to narrow as big is to **small**.
5. Hot is to cold as warm is to **cool**.
6. Slow is to fast as happy is to **sad**.
7. Dim is to bright as rich is to **poor**.
8. Stay is to leave as run is to **walk**.
9. Shy is to outgoing as quiet is to **loud**.
10. Stop is to start as quit is to **begin**.

Name _____   Vocabulary

Analogies

Analogies show relationships between words. For example, boy is to man as girl is to woman. The relationship between boy and man is the same as the relationship between girl and woman.

Find the missing word in each analogy below.

| year | puppy | healthy | wet | tale |
| lead | alert | yell | lower | messy |

1. Pen is to ink as pencil is to **lead**.
2. Cat is to kitten as dog is to **puppy**.
3. Asleep is to awake as tired is to **alert**.
4. Whisper is to shout as mumble is to **yell**.
5. Sick is to well as unhealthy is to **healthy**.
6. Clean is to dirty as neat is to **messy**.
7. Old is to young as dry is to **wet**.
8. Fact is to fiction as article is to **tale**.
9. Open is to shut as raise is to **lower**.
10. Day is to week as month is to **year**.

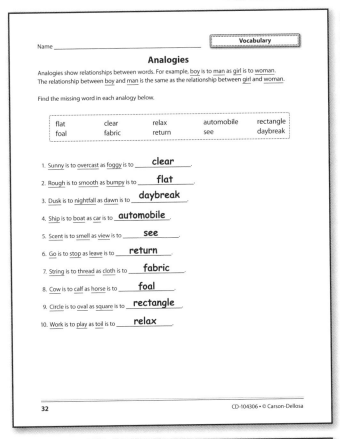

Name _____

Vocabulary

Analogies

Analogies show relationships between words. For example, boy is to man as girl is to woman. The relationship between boy and man is the same as the relationship between girl and woman.

Find the missing word in each analogy below.

| flat | clear | relax | automobile | rectangle |
| foal | fabric | return | see | daybreak |

1. Sunny is to overcast as foggy is to __clear__.
2. Rough is to smooth as bumpy is to __flat__.
3. Dusk is to nightfall as dawn is to __daybreak__.
4. Ship is to boat as car is to __automobile__.
5. Scent is to smell as view is to __see__.
6. Go is to stop as leave is to __return__.
7. String is to thread as cloth is to __fabric__.
8. Cow is to calf as horse is to __foal__.
9. Circle is to oval as square is to __rectangle__.
10. Work is to play as toil is to __relax__.

32   CD-104306 • © Carson-Dellosa

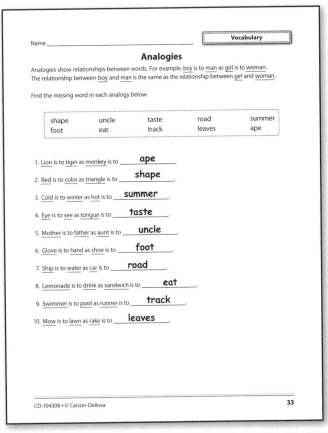

Name _____

Vocabulary

Analogies

Analogies show relationships between words. For example, boy is to man as girl is to woman. The relationship between boy and man is the same as the relationship between girl and woman.

Find the missing word in each analogy below.

| shape | uncle | taste | road | summer |
| foot | eat | track | leaves | ape |

1. Lion is to tiger as monkey is to __ape__.
2. Red is to color as triangle is to __shape__.
3. Cold is to winter as hot is to __summer__.
4. Eye is to see as tongue is to __taste__.
5. Mother is to father as aunt is to __uncle__.
6. Glove is to hand as shoe is to __foot__.
7. Ship is to water as car is to __road__.
8. Lemonade is to drink as sandwich is to __eat__.
9. Swimmer is to pool as runner is to __track__.
10. Mow is to lawn as rake is to __leaves__.

CD-104306 • © Carson-Dellosa   33

Name _____

Vocabulary

Analogies

Analogies show relationships between words. For example, boy is to man as girl is to woman. The relationship between boy and man is the same as the relationship between girl and woman.

Find the missing word in each analogy below.

| shorts | dresser | hot | draw | stroll |
| sip | sentence | feathers | princess | orchestra |

1. King is to queen as prince is to __princess__.
2. Winter is to coat as summer is to __shorts__.
3. Book is to chapter as paragraph is to __sentence__.
4. Leap is to jump as walk is to __stroll__.
5. Kitchen is to stove as bedroom is to __dresser__.
6. Pen is to write as pencil is to __draw__.
7. Ice is to cold as soup is to __hot__.
8. Eat is to bite as drink is to __sip__.
9. Student is to class as musician is to __orchestra__.
10. Snake is to scales as bird is to __feathers__.

34   CD-104306 • © Carson-Dellosa

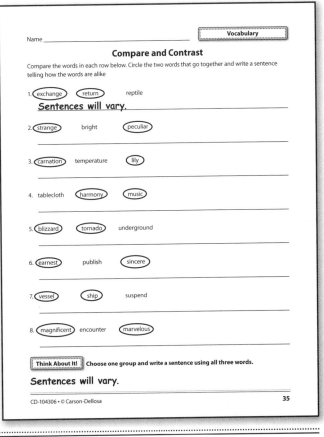

Name _____

Vocabulary

Compare and Contrast

Compare the words in each row below. Circle the two words that go together and write a sentence telling how the words are alike

1. (exchange) (return) reptile
   __Sentences will vary.__

2. (strange) bright (peculiar)

3. (carnation) temperature (lily)

4. tablecloth (harmony) (music)

5. (blizzard) (tornado) underground

6. (earnest) publish (sincere)

7. (vessel) (ship) suspend

8. (magnificent) encounter (marvelous)

Think About It! Choose one group and write a sentence using all three words.

__Sentences will vary.__

CD-104306 • © Carson-Dellosa   35

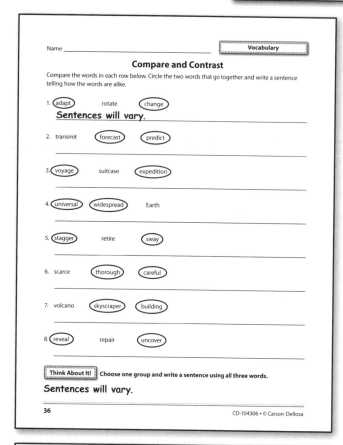

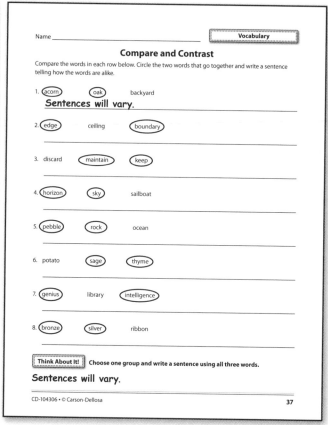

Name _____ Vocabulary

Compare and Contrast

Compare the words in each row below. Circle the two words that go together and write a sentence telling how the words are alike.

1. (adapt)   rotate   (change)
   Sentences will vary. _____

2. transmit   (forecast)   (predict)
   _____

3. (voyage)   suitcase   (expedition)
   _____

4. (universal)   (widespread)   Earth
   _____

5. (stagger)   retire   (sway)
   _____

6. scarce   (thorough)   (careful)
   _____

7. volcano   (skyscraper)   (building)
   _____

8. (reveal)   repair   (uncover)
   _____

Think About It! Choose one group and write a sentence using all three words.
Sentences will vary.

CD-104306 • © Carson-Dellosa

Name _____ Vocabulary

Compare and Contrast

Compare the words in each row below. Circle the two words that go together and write a sentence telling how the words are alike.

1. (acorn)   (oak)   backyard
   Sentences will vary. _____

2. (edge)   ceiling   (boundary)
   _____

3. discard   (maintain)   (keep)
   _____

4. (horizon)   (sky)   sailboat
   _____

5. (pebble)   (rock)   ocean
   _____

6. potato   (sage)   (thyme)
   _____

7. (genius)   library   (intelligence)
   _____

8. (bronze)   (silver)   ribbon
   _____

Think About It! Choose one group and write a sentence using all three words.
Sentences will vary.

CD-104306 • © Carson-Dellosa

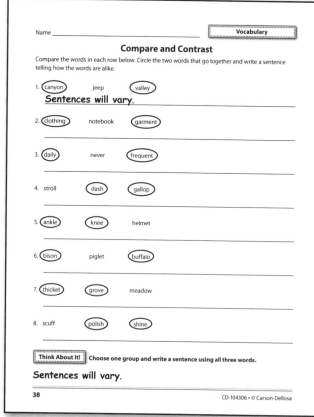

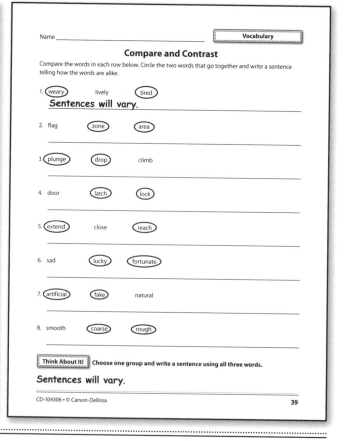

Name _____ Vocabulary

Compare and Contrast

Compare the words in each row below. Circle the two words that go together and write a sentence telling how the words are alike.

1. (canyon)   jeep   (valley)
   Sentences will vary. _____

2. (clothing)   notebook   (garment)
   _____

3. (daily)   never   (frequent)
   _____

4. stroll   (dash)   (gallop)
   _____

5. (ankle)   (knee)   helmet
   _____

6. (bison)   piglet   (buffalo)
   _____

7. (thicket)   (grove)   meadow
   _____

8. scuff   (polish)   (shine)
   _____

Think About It! Choose one group and write a sentence using all three words.
Sentences will vary.

CD-104306 • © Carson-Dellosa

Name _____ Vocabulary

Compare and Contrast

Compare the words in each row below. Circle the two words that go together and write a sentence telling how the words are alike.

1. (weary)   lively   (tired)
   Sentences will vary. _____

2. flag   (zone)   (area)
   _____

3. (plunge)   (drop)   climb
   _____

4. door   (latch)   (lock)
   _____

5. (extend)   close   (reach)
   _____

6. sad   (lucky)   (fortunate)
   _____

7. (artificial)   (fake)   natural
   _____

8. smooth   (coarse)   (rough)
   _____

Think About It! Choose one group and write a sentence using all three words.
Sentences will vary.

CD-104306 • © Carson-Dellosa

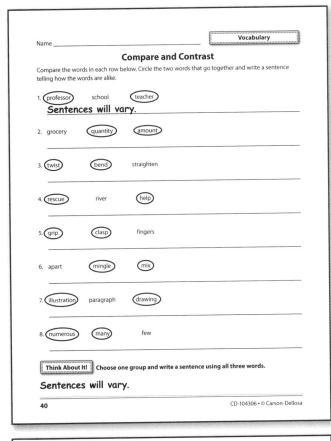

Name _____ Vocabulary

Compare and Contrast

Compare the words in each row below. Circle the two words that go together and write a sentence telling how the words are alike.

1. (professor)   school   (teacher)
   Sentences will vary.

2. grocery   (quantity)   (amount)

3. (twist)   (bend)   straighten

4. (rescue)   river   (help)

5. (grip)   (clasp)   fingers

6. apart   (mingle)   (mix)

7. (illustration)   paragraph   (drawing)

8. (numerous)   (many)   few

Think About It! Choose one group and write a sentence using all three words.
Sentences will vary.

40   CD-104306 • © Carson-Dellosa

Name _____ Reading about Symbolism

Read the story. Then, answer the questions.

What Are Symbols?

Symbols are things that stand for other things. We use symbols such as letters to stand for the sounds we make when we speak. The words made up by the letters stand for ideas. A symbol can tell how you feel about something. Your school might have a symbol such as a lion or a panther that stands for its teams. When you think of that animal, you feel pride in your school. Some symbols are used to stand for bigger things. The flag is a symbol of your country. A TV station might use a symbol to show the channel its programs are broadcast on. You can also see symbols in many buildings. Symbols help you know which restroom to use and which doors are accessible to people that use wheelchairs. These symbols are used as a kind of shorthand so that you can see the picture and quickly know what it means. Symbols are important in our everyday lives.

1. What is the main idea of this story?
   a. Symbols are important to our lives.
   b. Symbols can stand for animals.
   c. Symbols appear in many buildings.

2. What are symbols?
   things that stand for other things

3. Where might you see a symbol?
   Answers may vary.

4. Why might a school team use an animal as a symbol?
   Answers may vary.

5. Why might a TV station use a symbol?
   to show the channel its programs are broadcast on

6. Why are symbols important?
   Answers may vary.

CD-104306 • © Carson-Dellosa   41

Name _____ Reading about Symbolism

Read the story. Then, answer the questions.

Country Flags

Each country of the world uses a different flag. The flag tells something special about that country. It may have colors that are important to that country's people. It may have a picture of an important animal. The flag of the United States has 13 stripes and 50 stars. The stripes represent the original 13 colonies, and the stars stand for the 50 states in the country today. The flag of Canada has a maple leaf. There are many maple trees in Canada. The red leaf is shown on a white band between two bands of red. The flag of Mexico also has three bands of color, but in the middle is a picture that represents the settling of Mexico. The picture shows an eagle holding a snake in its claws, sitting on top of a cactus. According to legend, the first settlers of Mexico saw this bird in the area where they would build their first city. This city is now the capital of Mexico.

1. What is the main idea of this story?
   a. The Canadian flag has red and white areas.
   b. The first settlers of Mexico saw an eagle.
   c. Flags tell something special about a country.

2. Why does each country have its own flag?
   to tell something special about that country

3. What things might you find on a flag?
   colors, plants, or animals

4. What do the stripes and stars represent on the U.S. flag?
   stripes—original colonies, stars—current 50 states

5. What does the maple leaf mean on the Canadian flag?
   There are many maple trees in Canada.

6. Describe the flag of Mexico.
   three bands of color, with a picture in the middle of
   an eagle holding a snake in its claws and sitting on top
   of a cactus

42   CD-104306 • © Carson-Dellosa

Name _____ Reading about Symbolism

Read the story. Then, answer the questions.

Coats of Arms

A coat of arms is a special design used by a family or another group to show something special about that group. Coats of arms were used by knights in the Middle Ages to identify themselves. This design might be passed down through a family. A coat of arms often has an area called a "shield" in the middle. The shield may have different shapes or colors. Around the shield, there may be animals such as lions or eagles. Above the shield, there may be a special saying, such as "Knowledge and Honor." Countries sometimes use coats of arms as well. The Great Seal of the United States has many of the same elements as a coat of arms. It shows a bald eagle holding 13 arrows in one claw and an olive branch with 13 leaves in the other. The number of arrows and leaves stand for the 13 original states. The seal is used on important papers. It also appears on the U.S. one-dollar bill.

1. What is the main idea of this story?
   a. A coat of arms often has a shield on it.
   b. Coats of arms can stand for a family or another group.
   c. The Great Seal appears on the U.S. dollar bill.

2. What is a coat of arms?
   a special design used by a family or group to show
   something special about it

3. How were coats of arms used in the Middle Ages?
   They were used by knights to identify themselves.

4. What different things might appear on a shield?
   shapes and colors

5. What might appear above the shield?
   a special saying

6. Describe the Great Seal of the United States.
   a bald eagle holding 13 arrows in one claw and an
   olive branch with 13 leaves in the other

CD-104306 • © Carson-Dellosa   43

Flowers to Remember

Name _____ Reading about Symbolism

Read the story. Then, answer the questions.

Many countries have special days to remember different people. These days have special flowers connected with them as well. Mother's Day is celebrated in Canada and the United States on the second Sunday in May. Many people give carnations to their mothers on Mother's Day. The flower for Grandparents' Day, which is celebrated on the first Sunday after the U.S. Labor Day, in September, is a forget-me-not. These flowers are small and blue and have a yellow center. Another special day is Veterans Day. On this U.S. holiday, people honor the soldiers who have served in the military. In Canada, this holiday is Remembrance Day, because people *remember* those who have served. Both of these holidays are observed on November 11 every year. In Canada, people wear poppies on their coats. Poppies are red flowers with a black middle. The flowers stand for the poppies that bloomed over a French battlefield during World War I.

1. What is the main idea of this story?
   a. Some people wear poppies on their coats.
   b. Different flowers are worn on special holidays.
   c. Special days help us remember different people.

2. When is Mother's Day celebrated in the United States and Canada?
   on the second Sunday in May

3. What flowers are used for Mother's Day and Grandparents' Day?
   Mother's Day—carnations, Grandparents' Day—forget-me-nots

4. What does *remembrance* mean?
   a. a type of poppy
   b. people who have served in the military
   c. remembering someone or something

5. When are Veterans Day and Remembrance Day celebrated?
   November 11

6. What do the poppies worn on Remembrance Day stand for?
   the poppies that bloomed over a French battlefield during World War I

44   CD-104306 • © Carson-Dellosa

The Loon

Read the story. Then, answer the questions.

The loon is the state bird of Minnesota (United States) and the provincial bird of Ontario (Canada). Loons can be found in the northern part of the United States and throughout most of Canada. A loon is about the size of a large duck and has a dark head and checkered gray and white feathers. Loons dive for fish in lakes as deep as 200 feet (61 m) under the surface. They can swim for long distances underwater. Loons fly south to Mexico in the winter and come back north when the ice melts in the spring. In 1998, the Canadian postal service issued a special stamp worth one dollar that had a picture of a loon on it. The loon also appears on the Canadian dollar coin, which was introduced in 1987. This coin is often called the loonie. The Canadian two-dollar coin, introduced in 1996, features a polar bear. People call this coin the toonie.

1. What is the main idea of this story?
   a. Loons are special birds in Canada.
   b. Loons dive for fish underwater.
   c. The Canadian dollar coin is called the loonie.

2. Which U.S. state and Canadian province honor the loon?
   Minnesota and Ontario

3. Where are loons found?
   in the northern part of the United States and throughout Canada

4. What does a loon look like?
   It is the size of a large duck and has a dark head and checkered gray and white feathers.

5. How was the loon recognized in 1998?
   The Canadian postal service issued a stamp with a picture of the loon on it.

CD-104306 • © Carson-Dellosa   45

Birthday Symbols

Read the story. Then, answer the questions.

Many people recognize their birthdays by doing something special, such as inviting their friends over or having a family dinner. There are also special symbols that stand for the different months of the year, such as flowers and gemstones. Each of these also has a meaning connected with it. For example, the flower for March birthdays is the daffodil. This yellow flower represents happiness and friendship. The flower was chosen because it blooms during that month. Gemstones are another way of recognizing different birthday months. These pretty, sparkling rocks are polished and used to make jewelry. People might wear earrings, a necklace, or a pin with their birthstone in it. The gemstone for January is the deep red garnet stone. May's birthstone is an emerald, which is bright green. The most famous birthstone is probably the diamond, which stands for the month of April. On your next birthday, remember your special flower and gemstone too.

1. What is the main idea of this story?
   a. Stones and flowers always stand for the same thing.
   b. The daffodil is the flower for March.
   c. Each month has a special flower and stone.

2. What does the daffodil stand for?
   happiness and friendship

3. How are birthday flowers chosen?
   They are chosen based on the flowers blooming that month.

4. What are gemstones?
   a. polished rocks used in jewelry
   b. special kinds of flowers
   c. stones that are dull and gray

5. What do garnets and emeralds look like?
   garnets—deep red, emeralds—bright green

46   CD-104306 • © Carson-Dellosa

Animal Symbols

Read the story. Then, answer the questions.

Animals can mean different things to different people. To one family, a squirrel might be just a pest in the yard, but to another, a squirrel might serve as a reminder to put away food for the winter. A lion represents strength and courage, but it also stands for the country of Great Britain. It appears on the country's official coat of arms and reminds people of King Richard the Lionheart. The eagle stands for freedom, strength, and courage. It appears on the Great Seal of the United States and is also important in many American Indian cultures. Sports teams often choose an animal to represent them on the playing field. The team members remember their animal's qualities, such as speed and power, when they are playing. Some cars are also named after animals, such as a mustang or a ram, so that people will think the cars are as fast or as strong as those animals.

1. What is the main idea of this story?
   a. Animals are important symbols for different groups of people.
   b. Some cars are as fast as a mustang.
   c. Squirrels store food for the winter.

2. How might people see squirrels differently?
   Some people see them as pests, while some are reminded to put away food for the winter.

3. What does the lion stand for?
   strength and courage

4. What does the eagle stand for?
   freedom, strength, and courage

5. Why might a sports team choose an animal to represent it?
   so the members can remember that animal's qualities when they are playing

6. Why are some cars named after animals?
   so people will think the cars are like the animals

CD-104306 • © Carson-Dellosa   47

Name _____

Read the story. Then, answer the questions.

Political Parties

Political parties are groups of people who feel the same way about one or more issues. Each party may work to elect several candidates to office, from the president down to the city mayor. Political parties often use symbols to represent them. When people see that symbol, they will think of the party. The donkey was first used in a political ad to represent President Andrew Jackson, who was a Democrat. Donkeys can be smart and courageous. The U.S. Republican Party symbol is the elephant. Elephants are known for their strength and intelligence. Both of these parties use red, white, and blue—the colors of the U.S. flag. Many of the Canadian political parties have maple leaves as part of their logos, or designs. The maple leaf appears on the Canadian flag, so this shows that the parties are tied to their country. Political parties in Great Britain use different symbols. The Labor Party uses the rose (the national flower), the Conservative Party uses the oak tree (for strength), and the Liberal Democrats use a dove (for peace).

1. What is the main idea of this story?
   a. Political parties work to elect people to office.
   b. Political parties use symbols to represent them.
   c. The Canadian flag has a maple leaf on it.

2. What are political parties?
   groups of people who feel the same way about one or more issues

3. Why does the Democratic Party use a donkey?
   Answers may vary.

4. Why does the Republican Party use an elephant?
   Answers may vary.

5. Why might a political party use symbols from its country's flag?
   Answers may vary.

6. What are some symbols used by British political parties?
   rose, oak tree, dove

Name _____

Read the story. Then, answer the questions.

Symbols of Canadian Provinces

While Canada has many national symbols, such as the loon and the maple leaf, each of its provinces also has special symbols to represent it. Many of them have provincial plants, animals, and mottoes, or sayings. The province of Newfoundland and Labrador even has its own song! Alberta's official flower is the wild rose, and its bird is the great horned owl. Its motto is "strong and free," and its provincial fish is the bull trout. New Brunswick's flower is the purple violet. Its bird is the black-capped chickadee, and its tree is the balsam fir. Nova Scotia's official animal is a dog called the duck-tolling retriever. Its name means that it is good at finding ducks. Manitoba's bird is the great gray owl. Its official animal is the bison, and its tree is the white spruce. The province's motto is "glorious and free." Each province also has its own flag to show something about the history of that area.

1. What is the main idea of this story?
   a. Canadian provinces use symbols to tell something about them.
   b. Each province has its own flag.
   c. Canada has many national symbols.

2. What is a *motto*?
   a. an official flower
   b. a loon or a maple leaf
   c. a short saying that represents an idea

3. What is special about the province of Newfoundland and Labrador?
   It has its own provincial song.

4. List the provincial flowers for two Canadian provinces.
   Alberta—wild rose, New Brunswick—purple violet

5. List the provincial birds for two Canadian provinces.
   Answers may vary.

6. What does a provincial flag tell you about that province?
   something about the history of the area

Name _____

Read the story. Then, answer the questions.

U.S. State Symbols

The United States has many national symbols that represent liberty and freedom. Each U.S. state also has its own symbols, including state animals, flowers, and flags. The state of Washington has a picture of George Washington, the first U.S. president, on its flag. The state fruit is the apple, and the state vegetable is the Walla Walla sweet onion, which grows in the city of Walla Walla. Louisiana has a pelican, the state bird, on its flag. The state reptile is the alligator. Alaska's flag shows a pattern of stars known as the Big Dipper. The state fish is the king salmon, and the state mineral is gold. Ohio's state insect is the ladybug. The state tree is the buckeye. Texas is known as the Lone Star State because its flag has a single star on it. The state plant is the prickly pear cactus, and the state flower is the bluebonnet. Each state's symbols can tell you a lot about the plants and animals that live there.

1. What is the main idea of this story?
   a. National symbols represent liberty and freedom.
   b. U.S. states have many different symbols.
   c. The state tree of Ohio is the buckeye.

2. What are the state bird and reptile of Louisiana?
   bird—pelican, reptile—alligator

3. What does the Alaska flag look like?
   It has a pattern of stars known as the Big Dipper.

4. Why is Texas called the Lone Star State?
   Its flag has a single star on it.

5. What do a state's symbols tell you about it?
   They tell you about the plants and animals that live there.

Name _____

Read the story. Then, answer the questions.

Smiley Face

You have probably seen a bright yellow smiley face in an ad or on a sign. Some people even wear them on T-shirts! The smiley face was created in 1963 by an artist named Harvey Ball. Ball was asked to come up with a symbol for an insurance company to use. The company wanted employees to feel cheerful about working for the company when they saw the smiley face. Ball drew something very simple and made the background yellow because it reminded him of the sun. Soon, the symbol became so popular that thousands of people outside the company were wearing smiley face buttons. In the 1970s, the smiley face was put on T-shirts, coffee mugs, and bumper stickers. It has brought a smile to many people's faces around the world. Today, people sometimes use smiley faces in their e-mails to represent different feelings. Harvey Ball probably never thought his symbol would still be used over 40 years later.

1. What is the main idea of this story?
   a. The smiley face is still used today.
   b. Harvey Ball created the smiley face.
   c. The smiley face is a simple symbol that has been around for a long time.

2. Why was the smiley face created?
   An artist created the symbol for employees of an insurance company.

3. Why did Harvey Ball make the background yellow?
   because it reminded him of the sun

4. How was the smiley face used in the 1970s?
   It was put on T-shirts, coffee mugs, and bumper stickers.

5. How do people use the smiley face today?
   They use smiley faces in their e-mails to represent different feelings.

6. Why is the smiley face so popular?
   Answers may vary.

Answer Key

Name _____

Reading about Symbolism

Read the story. Then, answer the questions.

Colors

Colors can symbolize different things. When you see the color orange, you might feel happy because it reminds you of a sunny day. It might make you feel warm. When you see the color blue, you might feel calm because it makes you think of a still lake. It might make you feel cool to think of swimming in the water. When you see the colors green, brown, and blue together, you might think of the beauty of nature. These colors are used on world globes. Colors can also be used to alert us to danger. Fire trucks are red so that people will notice them and move out of the way. Stoplights use colors to tell cars whether to move. A red light signals to stop, a green light signals to go, and a yellow light signals to yield, or to slow down and be more careful. Pay attention to the colors around you. They might help you in ways you do not expect.

1. What is the main idea of this story?
   - (a.) Colors can mean many different things.
   - b. A still lake might make you feel calm.
   - c. Pay attention to the colors around you.

2. What does the color orange make you think of?
   Answers may vary.

3. What does the color blue make you think of?
   Answers may vary.

4. Why might green, brown, and blue make you think of nature?
   because they are the colors used on world globes

5. Why are fire trucks red?
   so people will notice them and move out of the way

6. What do the colors on a stoplight mean?
   red—stop, green—go, yellow—slow down and be more careful

52   CD-104306 • © Carson-Dellosa

Name _____

Reading about Science

Read the story. Then, answer the questions.

Plant Parts

Plants have many parts. You can see some of them, and there are parts you cannot see. The plant begins with the root system underground. It sends out long, thin roots into the soil to gather water and minerals. The part of the plant that grows out of the ground is called the stem. The stem moves water and minerals from the soil up into the leaves. Sunlight helps the leaves make more food, which is moved to other parts of the plant. The leaves also produce the oxygen in the air we breathe. Some leaves have only one broad, flat area connected to the stem. Others have many leaflets, or slim, needle-like parts. Many plants have flowers at the top of the stem. The petals of a flower help attract bees and butterflies, which bring pollen from other flowers. The pollen helps the flower make new plants the next year. Some plants produce fruit. When the seeds in the middle of the fruit are planted, a new plant can grow.

1. What is the main idea of this story?
   - a. A plant's root system is underground.
   - (b.) Plants have parts such as roots, leaves, and petals.
   - c. Bees and butterflies like flowers.

2. How does the root system help the plant?
   It brings water and minerals from the soil to the stem.

3. What do leaves need to make food for the plant?
   water, minerals, and sunlight

4. Describe two ways that leaves can look.
   broad and flat or slim and needle-like

5. How do the petals of a flower help the plant?
   They attract bees and butterflies, which bring pollen.

6. What happens when seeds from fruit are planted?
   A new plant can grow.

CD-104306 • © Carson-Dellosa   53

Name _____

Reading about Science

Read the story. Then, answer the questions.

Ecosystems

All living plants and animals live in ecosystems. An ecosystem can be as large as Earth or as small as a puddle. A lizard might live in a desert ecosystem. A whale would live in an ocean ecosystem. In an ecosystem, all of the living things, such as plants and animals, and nonliving things, such as the soil and the weather, work together. Changing even one thing will affect the other parts of the ecosystem. For example, if the ecosystem where frogs live becomes polluted, the frogs may become sick. If something happens to the frogs, then the animals that eat them, such as snakes, will not have enough food. If there is a fire in a forest, then the mosses on the forest floor will not have shade to grow in. The ecosystem will change from one with large trees and plants that need cool temperatures to one with plants that do well with more sunlight. People must try to protect the ecosystems in which they live. It is important to remember that even if you cannot see every organism in the ecosystem, everything is connected.

1. What is the main idea of this story?
   - (a.) In an ecosystem, everything is connected.
   - b. Some ecosystems are forests, and some are deserts.
   - c. Ecosystems can be large or small.

2. Name three types of ecosystems.
   Answers may vary.

3. What happens if one thing is changed in an ecosystem?
   The other parts can change too.

4. What might happen if frogs in an ecosystem disappeared?
   The animals that eat them would have nothing to eat.

5. What might happen after a forest fire?
   The mosses on the forest floor would not have shade to grow in. The ecosystem would change into one with plants that need more sunlight.

6. Why is it important to protect ecosystems?
   Answers may vary.

54   CD-104306 • © Carson-Dellosa

Name _____

Reading about Science

Read the story. Then, answer the questions.

The Atmosphere

The atmosphere is the air that surrounds Earth. The air you breathe is part of the atmosphere. Earth's atmosphere contains the gases oxygen, nitrogen, and argon, along with dust, pollen, and water. Oxygen is the most important part of the atmosphere. It is made by plants during their food-making process. In addition to breathing the atmosphere, you can also feel it. When you feel a cool breeze in autumn or warm air on a summer day, you are feeling the atmosphere. The atmosphere has different layers. The troposphere is the layer above the surface of Earth. The troposphere makes up half the atmosphere. All weather occurs in this layer. The next layer is the stratosphere, where jets often fly. This layer absorbs much of the sun's harmful rays. In the mesosphere, the third layer of the atmosphere, rocks from space are caught and burned. The space shuttle orbits in the next layer, the thermosphere. The last layer is the exosphere. After that, you are out in space!

1. What is the main idea of this story?
   - a. Air is made up of many gases.
   - b. A cool breeze is part of the atmosphere.
   - (c.) The atmosphere surrounds Earth and provides us with air.

2. What does Earth's atmosphere contain?
   gases such as oxygen, nitrogen, and argon, and dust, pollen, and water

3. What are two ways you can feel the atmosphere?
   as a cool autumn breeze or warm air on a summer day

4. List the layers of the atmosphere.
   troposphere, stratosphere, mesosphere, thermosphere, exosphere

5. What important thing happens in the stratosphere?
   The sun's harmful rays are absorbed.

6. In which layers of the atmosphere might you find man-made flying objects?
   troposphere, stratosphere, thermosphere

CD-104306 • © Carson-Dellosa   55

Answer Key

Name _____

Read the story. Then, answer the questions.

Climate

The climate describes the weather in an area over a long period of time. If you live somewhere where there are large amounts of yearly rainfall, then you live in a rainy climate. If your town is very hot and dry, then you may live in a desert climate. Some cities, such as San Diego, California, have a very mild climate. Others, such as New Orleans, Louisiana, have warm, heavy air, so they have a humid climate. While the weather in a place may change from day to day, a region's climate seldom changes. Factors other than weather can also affect the climate in a given area. Areas that are close to the sea are cooler and wetter. They may also be cloudy, because clouds form when warm inland air meets the cooler air from the sea. Mountains may also affect climate. Because the temperature at the top of a mountain is cooler than at the ground level, the mountaintop may have year-round snow. Regions near Earth's middle, or equator, are warmer than those at the poles. Sunlight has farther to travel to get to the north and south poles, so these areas are much cooler.

1. What is the main idea of this story?
   - a. Climate is the weather in a place over a long period of time.
   - b. The north and south poles are very cold.
   - c. Some climates are rainy, and some are very hot.

2. How are the climates of San Diego and New Orleans different?
   San Diego—mild, New Orleans—humid

3. What is the difference between weather and climate?
   Weather can change often, while climate is the weather in an area over a long period of time.

4. What climate might a city by the sea have?
   cool, wet, and cloudy

5. What climate might be found on a mountain?
   snowy and cold

6. How are climates near the equator different from those at the poles?
   Climates near the equator are warmer.

56   CD-104306 • © Carson-Dellosa

Name _____

Read the story. Then, answer the questions.

Comets

Comets are objects that look like dirty snowballs flying through space. They have tails of dust that may be over 6 million miles (10 million km) long. Besides the tail, a comet has a nucleus, or center, made up of a closely packed ball of ice and dust. Surrounding the nucleus is a cloud of water and gases referred to as the coma. People can see comets only when they pass close to the sun. As they get closer to the sun, some of the ice in the nucleus melts, forming the long tail. Some comets appear after regular periods of time. Halley's Comet, named after Edmond Halley, the person who first predicted its return, passes through the solar system every 76 years. It was last seen in 1986 and will appear again in 2062. Earth is in no danger from comets. When the planet passes through the comet's tail, small pieces of rock called meteors fall into the atmosphere. Most of these are burned up in the mesosphere. They appear during a meteor shower as shooting stars.

1. What is the main idea of this story?
   - a. Halley's Comet is very famous.
   - b. Comets are objects from outer space made up of dust and ice.
   - c. Comets are not dangerous to Earth.

2. Describe the parts of a comet.
   nucleus, or center—closely packed ball of ice and dust, coma—cloud of water and gases, tail—water and pieces of dust

3. What happens as a comet gets closer to the sun?
   Some of the ice in the nucleus melts, forming the long tail.

4. Who was Edmond Halley?
   the person who first predicted the comet's return

5. What is a meteor?
   - a. a comet that passes by every 76 years
   - b. ice from the comet's nucleus
   - c. a small piece of rock from space

6. What happens when Earth passes through a comet's tail?
   Meteors fall into the atmosphere and are burned up.

CD-104306 • © Carson-Dellosa   57

Name _____

Read the story. Then, answer the questions.

Vaccinations

Some people go to the doctor for shots called vaccinations. Vaccinations can protect people and animals from diseases. The first vaccination was developed by Edward Jenner, who was looking for a way to prevent smallpox in the late 1700s. Vaccinations work by injecting a dead or weak part of the disease into a person or animal. The body makes antibodies to fight the disease, and the person or animal then becomes immune to that disease. This means that they will not develop the disease, or they will have only a very mild form of it. The most important animal vaccine is for the disease rabies. Many cities require that people vaccinate their pets so that none of them will catch the disease from a wild animal. Some people build natural antibodies to the diseases in their area. If you visit another country, you may be required to get a vaccination for a disease that exists in that country. People who live there might have natural antibodies to the disease, but a visitor might not. Vaccinations can help build antibodies to diseases with which you would not normally come into contact.

1. What is the main idea of this story?
   - a. Doctors give vaccinations.
   - b. The first vaccination was developed by Edward Jenner.
   - c. Vaccinations can help keep people and animals healthy.

2. What disease was the first vaccination developed to prevent?
   smallpox

3. How do vaccinations work?
   A dead or weak part of the disease is injected, and the body makes antibodies to fight the disease.

4. What does it mean to become *immune* to something?
   - a. to get a shot at the doctor's office
   - b. to have little chance of getting sick from a disease
   - c. to visit another country

5. Why might you need a vaccination when you visit another country?
   because you might not have natural antibodies against the diseases found there

58   CD-104306 • © Carson-Dellosa

Name _____

Read the story. Then, answer the questions.

Biofuels

Gasoline is used in cars, and oil is used to heat many homes. Biofuels have similar uses, but they are made from things like vegetable oil, which can be recycled and used again. Diesel is a type of fuel similar to heating oil. Diesel is used in cars and trucks. Biodiesel, most of which is made from soybean oil, burns more cleanly than diesel. It can be used in diesel engines without having to add any special parts. Biodiesel produces less pollution, so it is better for the environment. Gasoline is known as a fossil fuel, which means that it comes from layers deep under the earth that are made up of plants and animals that lived millions of years ago. Biofuel comes from plants we grow today, so it is a renewable resource. Some biofuels are created from restaurants' leftover grease that was used to make foods such as french fries or fried chicken. Instead of throwing this grease away, people are finding ways to power their cars with it.

1. What is the main idea of this story?
   - a. Biofuels are better for the environment than fossil fuels.
   - b. Gasoline and diesel are used to power cars.
   - c. Some people throw grease away after cooking.

2. What are biofuels?
   fuels made from things that can be recycled and used again

3. Why might people choose to use biodiesel rather than diesel fuel?
   It burns more cleanly and is better for the environment.

4. What is a fossil fuel?
   - a. fuel used in cars and trucks
   - b. grease used to make fried foods
   - c. fuel made from plants and animals from long ago

5. What is a renewable resource?
   something that can be used or grown again

6. What are some things used to make biofuels?
   vegetable oil, soybean oil, grease from fried foods

CD-104306 • © Carson-Dellosa   59

Answer Key

Name _____

Read the story. Then, answer the questions.

Endangered Species

Many species of animals around the world are endangered today. This means that there are very few of them left. Species sometimes become endangered through loss of habitat, as when a wilderness area is changed by building a city there. They may also become endangered when people hunt them for food or for their skin. Many countries keep lists of the species that live there and are endangered. People can work to protect these species' environments from further loss. They can also move animals to zoos or nature preserves to try to increase their numbers. When they think it is safe again, they will reintroduce the animal to its native habitat. The alligator was once on the U.S. Endangered Species List because many people liked to make shoes or purses from its tough hide. After a law was passed making it illegal to kill alligators, the number of alligators in the wild increased. In 1987, it was removed from the list. The alligator is an endangered species success story!

1. What is the main idea of this story?
   a. Many countries keep lists of endangered species.
   b. Areas can be changed when cities are built there.
   c. **Many species of animals around the world are endangered.**

2. What does it mean for an animal to be endangered?
   It means that there are very few of them left.

3. How do species become endangered?
   through habitat loss or overhunting for food or for their skin

4. How do people work to protect species?
   by protecting their environments from further loss and moving the animals to zoos or nature preserves

5. When do people take animals back to their native habitat?
   when it is safe again or their numbers have increased

6. Why was the alligator removed from the U.S. Endangered Species List?
   because its numbers increased after a law was passed to make it illegal to kill alligators

CD-104306 • © Carson-Dellosa

Name _____

Read the story. Then, answer the questions.

Volcanoes

Volcanoes are special mountains that sometimes shoot a hot liquid called lava into the air. Beneath a volcano is a pool of molten, or melted, rock. When the pressure underground builds up, the liquid is forced upward and out of the cone, or top, of the volcano. The liquid inside the volcano is called magma, but when it reaches the surface it is referred to as lava. A lava flow may travel down the sides of the volcano and over the land for several miles. As lava gets farther from the top of the volcano, it cools down and moves more slowly. Volcanic eruptions can be very harmful. Ash is sent into the air and can make it difficult to breathe. Rocks and lava from the eruption can flatten everything around the volcano, including forests and towns. Most volcanoes in the United States are located along the West Coast and in Hawaii and Alaska. The world's largest active volcano is in Mauna Loa, Hawaii. Another region of the world with many volcanoes is in the Pacific Ocean. This area is known as the Ring of Fire.

1. What is the main idea of this story?
   a. The Ring of Fire is located in the Pacific Ocean.
   b. **Volcanoes shoot lava into the air and can be very dangerous.**
   c. Lava flows can reach for miles around a volcano.

2. What is the *cone* of the volcano?
   a. **the top, where lava shoots out**
   b. the pool of molten rock underneath the earth
   c. the area around the volcano

3. What is the difference between magma and lava?
   Magma is liquid inside the volcano; it is called lava when it reaches the surface.

4. How can volcanoes be dangerous?
   They can shoot ash into the air, making it hard to breathe, and the rocks and lava can flatten forests and towns around the volcano.

5. Where are most volcanoes in the United States located?
   along the West Coast and in Hawaii and Alaska

CD-104306 • © Carson-Dellosa

Name _____

Read the story. Then, answer the questions.

Simple Machines

When you think of the word *machine*, you may picture a car engine or a lawnmower. These machines have many moving parts. Simple machines are tools that people use to make their work easier. They have very few parts. Instead of electric power, they use the energy of people to work. One simple machine is a lever. A lever is a board that rests on a turning point that makes it easier to lift things. A seesaw is a lever. Students on a seesaw use the board to make it easier to lift each other. Another simple machine is an inclined plane. To *incline* something means "to lean it against something else." An inclined plane is a flat surface that is higher on one end than the other. A ramp is an inclined plane. You might use a ramp to wheel a cart up to a curb instead of having to lift it. A slide is another inclined plane. Simple machines can make our lives easier in ways that are simple yet important.

1. What is the main idea of this story?
   a. Car engines and lawnmowers have many parts.
   b. A seesaw is a type of simple machine.
   c. **Simple machines can make our lives much easier.**

2. What do simple machines use instead of electricity?
   the energy of people

3. What is a lever?
   a board that rests on a turning point that makes it easier to lift things

4. What does it mean to *incline*?
   a. **lean at an angle**
   b. use a simple machine
   c. play on a seesaw

5. What is an inclined plane?
   a flat surface that is higher on one end than the other

6. What are two examples of simple machines?
   Answers may vary.

CD-104306 • © Carson-Dellosa

Name _____

Read the story. Then, answer the questions.

Rainbows

You may have seen a rainbow in the sky after a rainstorm. A rainbow includes the colors red, orange, yellow, green, blue, indigo, and violet. You can remember the order of the colors with the name Roy G. Biv. All of the colors combined create white light. A rainbow is formed when a ray of sunlight shines through a cloud, refracts off the water droplets, and is split into bands of color. Rainbows are fairly rare to see. This is because special conditions are required for them to become visible. To see a rainbow, you must have rain in front of you, at a distance, and the sun behind you, low on the horizon. The curve of the rainbow is in the direction opposite from the sun. Rainbows are more common in summertime, because you must have both rain and warm sunlight to see them. Because there is less sunlight and more frozen water, rainbows are less likely to form during winter.

1. What is the main idea of this story?
   a. **Rainbows are formed when light is split into bands.**
   b. Rainbows are very rare.
   c. Rainbows have many colors in them.

2. What does Roy G. Biv stand for?
   red, orange, yellow, green, blue, indigo, violet

3. What do all the colors combined create?
   white light

4. How is a rainbow formed?
   when sunlight refracts off the water in a cloud and is split into bands of color

5. Why are rainbows rare to see?
   because the rain must be in front of you and the sun must be behind you

6. Why are rainbows more common in the summertime?
   because you need sunshine and rain to see them

CD-104306 • © Carson-Dellosa

Name _____

Reading about Science

Read the story. Then, answer the questions.

Atoms and Molecules

Everything around you is called matter—from your chair to your clothes to your family. Matter is made up of atoms and molecules, which are very tiny building blocks. Atoms make up chemical elements, such as the oxygen in the air you breathe. Atoms are combined to create molecules, such as the water you drink. Atoms are composed of even smaller particles called protons, neutrons, and electrons. A proton has a positive charge, an electron has a negative charge, and a neutron has no charge. The protons and neutrons stay together in the nucleus, or middle, while the electrons orbit, or move around, the atom. The number of protons determines the type of atom that is formed. Hydrogen is the simplest atom. It has only one proton. Oxygen has eight protons. Together, hydrogen and oxygen can form a molecule of water. Each water molecule has two hydrogen atoms and one oxygen atom. A glass of water contains too many molecules to count!

1. What is the main idea of this story?
   a. Atoms combine to make molecules.
   b. All matter is made up of atoms and molecules.
   c. A glass of water contains many molecules.

2. What are two examples of atoms?
   oxygen, hydrogen

3. What does *orbit* mean?
   a. stay in the middle
   b. a type of molecule
   c. move around something

4. Describe the differences between protons, neutrons, and electrons.
   protons—positive charge, stay in nucleus; neutrons—no charge, stay in nucleus; electrons—negative charge, orbit nucleus

5. Why is hydrogen the simplest atom?
   because it has only one proton

6. What is a water molecule made up of?
   two hydrogen atoms and one oxygen atom

64   CD-104306 • © Carson-Dellosa

Name _____

Reading about Science

Read the story. Then, answer the questions.

Bacteria

Your family or teachers may have told you to wash your hands with soap and hot water. This is to avoid the spread of bacteria. Bacteria are tiny organisms that live in your body and in the air, water, and soil. Bacteria are visible under a microscope. It would take one million bacteria to cover the head of a single pin! Bacteria may be small, but they can be very powerful. Some bacteria can cause infections such as a sore throat or cavities in your teeth. Not all bacteria are harmful, though. Your body has some good bacteria that help it digest food. Without bacteria, your intestines would not be able to gain the nutrition that they need from food and get rid of the waste that they do not need. Some bacteria are also used by scientists to make medicine and vaccines. In addition, they are used to make food such as cheese and yogurt. You should always wash your hands to ensure that you do not spread bad bacteria, but remember that some bacteria are good too.

1. What is the main idea of this story?
   a. Some bacteria are good, and some are bad.
   b. You should wash your hands before eating.
   c. Bacteria can be found in the air and the water.

2. Why should you wash your hands with soap and hot water?
   to avoid spreading any bad bacteria

3. What are two types of infections that bacteria can cause?
   sore throat, cavities in teeth

4. What do good bacteria in the body do?
   help digest food by gaining the nutrition needed and getting rid of the waste

5. How do scientists use bacteria?
   to make medicine and vaccines

6. What foods are bacteria used to make?
   cheese and yogurt

CD-104306 • © Carson-Dellosa   65

Name _____

Reading about Science

Read the story. Then, answer the questions.

The Tundra

The tundra is a special type of land found in extremely cold areas such as the Arctic and parts of Alaska and Canada. The tundra is sometimes referred to as a frozen desert. In areas with tundra, the ground is frozen the whole year. This permanently frozen ground is called permafrost. Very short shrubs grow in the tundra. It is difficult for taller plants to grow because the ground is so cold and hard. The tundra can be very windy because there is so little to block the wind. Wind speeds can reach nearly 60 miles (about 100 kilometers) per hour. Few animals live in the tundra because there are not many plants. However, many birds and insects travel there in the summertime when the ice on the marshes and lakes melts. Because of the cold, windy conditions, it is difficult for people to live in areas with tundra. Some scientists work on research stations for part of the year to study the plants and animals that live there.

1. What is the main idea of this story?
   a. The tundra is very cold and windy.
   b. Some scientists live in the tundra.
   c. The tundra has difficult living conditions for animals and plants.

2. Where can the tundra be found?
   in very cold areas such as the Arctic and parts of Alaska and Canada

3. What is permafrost?
   ground that is permanently frozen

4. Why is it hard for plants to grow in the tundra?
   because the ground is so cold and hard

5. Why do birds and insects travel to the tundra in the summertime?
   because the ice on the lakes and marshes melts then

6. What do some scientists do in the tundra?
   They work on research stations to study the plants and animals that live there.

66   CD-104306 • © Carson-Dellosa

Name _____

Reading about Science

Read the story. Then, answer the questions.

Salmon

Animals such as dogs and cats may spend their entire lives in the same city or town in which they were born. Other animals, however, travel great distances during their life cycle. The salmon swims from the rivers of Alaska to the Pacific Ocean and back again. The salmon lays its eggs in the riverbed. After about three months, the eggs hatch. Then, the tiny fish swim around the rivers until they are large enough to travel to the sea. As the fish grow older and larger, they develop patterns that look like finger marks along their sides. Once they are one to three years old, they move in groups toward the ocean. Their bodies change so they can live in salt water instead of freshwater. The young salmon then spend several years swimming in the ocean. Eventually, they will swim back to the river in which they were born. There they lay eggs, and the cycle begins again.

1. What is the main idea of this story?
   a. Salmon travel great distances over their life cycle.
   b. Some animals may live in the same city their whole lives.
   c. Salmon lay eggs in streams or rivers.

2. Where do salmon travel during their life cycle?
   from the rivers of Alaska to the Pacific Ocean and back again

3. How long does it take for salmon eggs to hatch?
   about three months

4. How does the salmon's body change as it grows older?
   It develops patterns that look like finger marks along its sides, and its body changes so it can live in saltwater instead of freshwater.

5. What happens when the salmon are one to three years old?
   They move in groups toward the ocean.

6. Where does the salmon go to lay its eggs?
   to the river in which it was born

CD-104306 • © Carson-Dellosa   67

Name _____

Read the story. Then, answer the questions.

The Aztecs

The Aztec people lived in the area that is now central Mexico. The Aztec Empire lasted from about 1325 to 1521 and stretched from the Pacific Ocean to the Gulf of Mexico. The Aztecs had a strong central government that was headed by a king or emperor. Under him were officials who governed different parts of the empire. The Aztecs enjoyed many foods, including corn or maize, beans, squash, tomatoes, and chili peppers. They sometimes added tomatoes and chili peppers. People in Mexico still eat many of these foods today. The Aztecs built temples that were similar to the Egyptian pyramids but without the pointed tops. On the outside of the temples were steps to the top, where there was a flat area. The Aztec people are known for their pottery and statues. They also made beautiful feathered headdresses, masks, shields, and clothing for their rulers to wear and use. You can find examples of Aztec crafts in museums today.

1. What is the main idea of this story?
   a. The Aztec people lived in the area that is now called Mexico.
   b. The Aztecs had a strong government and made many crafts.
   c. Aztec temples are like the Egyptian pyramids.

2. How long did the Aztec Empire last?
   about 200 years

3. How was the Aztec government organized?
   a central government headed by a king or emperor with officials under him who governed different parts of the empire

4. How are Aztec temples different from Egyptian pyramids?
   Aztec temples have steps on the outside and do not have a pointed top.

5. What kinds of crafts did the Aztecs make?
   pottery, statues, and feathered headdresses, masks, shields, and clothing

68   CD-104306 • © Carson-Dellosa

Name _____

Read the story. Then, answer the questions.

The Mississippi River

The Mississippi River is an important river for trade, recreation, and culture. It runs all the way from the U.S. state of Minnesota down to the Gulf of Mexico and covers 2,340 miles (3,770 km). The name *Mississippi* comes from an American Indian word meaning "great river." The first European explorer to reach the Mississippi was Hernando de Soto of Spain, who came there in 1541. In 1682 a group of French explorers claimed the river for their country. The city of New Orleans was built near the river in 1718. The United States acquired the area with the Louisiana Purchase of 1803. The Mississippi gained fame with the books of Mark Twain, which described life on the river. Twain, whose real name was Samuel Clemens, worked on a steamboat on the river in the late 1850s. Boats still travel down the Mississippi today, but people also water-ski and fish there. In addition, there are seven National Park Service areas along the river where people can go to enjoy nature.

1. What is the main idea of this story?
   a. The Mississippi River was made famous by Mark Twain.
   b. The Mississippi River was discovered by a Spanish explorer.
   c. The Mississippi River is important in many ways.

2. How long is the Mississippi?
   2,340 miles or 3,770 kilometers

3. Where did the Mississippi get its name?
   from an American Indian word meaning "great river"

4. Which countries' explorers visited the Mississippi?
   Spain and France

5. Who was Samuel Clemens?
   an author who went by the name Mark Twain and worked on a steamboat on the Mississippi in the late 1850s

6. What do people do on and around the Mississippi today?
   travel on boats, water-ski, fish, and visit national parks

CD-104306 • © Carson-Dellosa   69

Name _____

Read the story. Then, answer the questions.

Citizen Rights and Responsibilities

People who are citizens of a country have certain rights that belong to them. These rights are sometimes listed in the laws of that country. In Canada and the United States, citizens over the age of 18 are given the right to vote. Citizens also have the right to a fair trial and the right to speak freely about what they believe. They can practice any religion they want to, and they have the right to gather peacefully to exchange ideas. They have the right to ask their government to change laws that they think are wrong. With these rights come responsibilities too. People should obey the laws of their country. They should respect the opinions of others, even if they disagree with them. They should help others in their community and try to protect their environment. It is important to remember that all citizens are part of a large community and that everyone deserves to be treated fairly.

1. What is the main idea of this story?
   a. All citizens of a country have rights and responsibilities.
   b. Citizens have the right to vote.
   c. Everyone should be treated fairly in a community.

2. Where can you find a list of citizens' rights?
   in a country's laws

3. How old must citizens be to vote in Canada and the United States?
   18

4. What are three rights in Canada and the United States?
   Answers may vary.

5. What are three responsibilities in Canada and the United States?
   Answers may vary.

6. Why is it important to treat all citizens fairly?
   Answers may vary.

70   CD-104306 • © Carson-Dellosa

Name _____

Read the story. Then, answer the questions.

Explorers of Canada

The first people known to have reached Canada from Europe were the Vikings, who sailed from Norway across the Atlantic Ocean around the year 1000. John Cabot traveled to Canada from Great Britain in the late 1490s. He was trying to reach Asia but instead found North America. Jacques Cartier sailed to Canada from France later in the 1500s and discovered the St. Lawrence River, which flows from the Atlantic Ocean to the Great Lakes. Samuel de Champlain came from France in the 1600s to explore the area that is now known as Quebec. He made 12 trips to the area he called New France, and he started the first permanent settlement at Quebec City. George Vancouver came from Great Britain in the late 1700s to explore North America. He mapped the entire western coastline, all the way from the Gulf of Mexico to southern Alaska! Both Vancouver Island and the city of Vancouver are named after him.

1. What is the main idea of this story?
   a. Sometimes areas are named after the people who explored them.
   b. The Vikings were the first to explore Canada.
   c. Many people have explored Canada throughout the ages.

2. What was John Cabot trying to do when he sailed to Canada?
   He was trying to reach Asia.

3. What did Jacques Cartier discover?
   the St. Lawrence River

4. Where was New France?
   Quebec

5. How was George Vancouver honored for his discoveries?
   Both Vancouver Island and the city of Vancouver were named after him.

6. Which countries sent explorers to Canada or North America?
   Norway, France, and Great Britain

CD-104306 • © Carson-Dellosa   71

Name _____

Read the story. Then, answer the questions.

Becoming a U.S. State

There are 50 states in the United States today. The last states to be added were Alaska and Hawaii, in 1959. Most states admitted to the Union after the original 13 were U.S. territories first. To become a state, the people of the territory had to band together with an organized government and then write a state constitution. After the U.S. Congress accepted the constitution, that territory became a state. Areas that might become U.S. states someday include the island of Puerto Rico and the District of Columbia. While people who live in these areas now are U.S. citizens, they have limited voting rights. Puerto Rico has a resident commissioner instead of a senator, and the District of Columbia has a non-voting member of the U.S. House of Representatives. Each of the 50 U.S. states has two senators and one or more representatives in Congress. Some people who live in areas of the United States that are not states believe they need a greater say in Congress. Others would like to keep their independence.

1. What is the main idea of this story?
   (a.) Becoming a U.S. state allows people living there to have a say in the national government.
   b. Puerto Rico and the District of Columbia are not states.
   c. Each state sends several people to Congress.

2. What were the last states to be added? When?
   Alaska and Hawaii, in 1959

3. How does a U.S. territory become a state?
   The people living there form a government and write a constitution, which is then approved by the U.S. Congress.

4. How are U.S. territories different from U.S. states?
   People in U.S. territories do not send voting members to Congress.

5. How many members of Congress does each state have?
   at least three—two senators and at least one representative

6. Why might someone living in a U.S. territory want statehood?
   so they can vote for members of Congress

CD-104306 • © Carson-Dellosa

Name _____

Read the story. Then, answer the questions.

The Economy

You may have heard your family or a newscaster discuss the economy. The economy is a system in which goods and services are exchanged for money. Goods are things that are produced, such as books and clothing. Services are things people do for each other. For example, a teacher provides the service of educating students, and a police officer provides the service of keeping the community safe. Sometimes people provide a service that produces a good, such as a cook who prepares a meal that you can eat. People pay money for goods and services. When you give money to a producer of goods, she can purchase materials to make more goods. When you give money to a service provider, he may pay for more training to do his job better. They can also use the money to pay for basic items such as food and shelter. When newscasters report that the economy is strong, it means that most people are happy with the amount of money, goods, and services they have.

1. What is the main idea of this story?
   a. Newscasters often talk about the economy.
   b. Sometimes the economy is strong, and other times it is weak.
   (c.) The economy is a system in which goods and services are exchanged for money.

2. What are goods?
   things that are produced

3. List two examples of goods.
   Answers may vary.

4. What is a service?
   things people do for each other

5. List two examples of service providers.
   Answers may vary.

6. What does it mean when newscasters say the economy is strong?
   Most people are happy with the amount of money, goods, and services they have.

CD-104306 • © Carson-Dellosa

Name _____

Read the story. Then, answer the questions.

World Holidays

People around the world celebrate different holidays. Both Canada and the United States have special days to mark the countries' birthdays. Canada Day is celebrated on July 1, and Independence Day in the United States is celebrated on July 4. On both of these holidays, people may have parades or picnics with their families. Many holidays have special foods associated with them. People may eat turkey on Thanksgiving or chocolate on Valentine's Day. During the Chinese New Year, people eat sticky rice dumplings. This holiday comes at the beginning of the Chinese New Year, in January or February, and has been celebrated for over 1,000 years! People in many other countries celebrate New Year's Eve on December 31. It is common for people to sing an old Scottish song called "Auld Lang Syne," which can be translated as "for old times' sake." They sing the song to remember the good times of the past and to look forward to more good times in the future.

1. What is the main idea of this story?
   a. Canada Day is celebrated on July 1.
   (b.) People around the world celebrate different holidays.
   c. Some people eat turkey at Thanksgiving.

2. How are Canada Day and Independence Day similar?
   Both mark a country's birthday, both are celebrated in July, and people celebrate in similar ways.

3. What are some foods eaten at holidays?
   turkey, chocolate, sticky rice dumplings

4. What festival is held at the Chinese New Year?
   the Chinese Lantern Festival

5. When is the Chinese New Year celebrated? When do other people celebrate the New Year?
   January or February; December 31

6. Why do people sing "Auld Lang Syne"?
   to remember the good times of the past and to look forward to more good times in the future

CD-104306 • © Carson-Dellosa

Name _____

Read the story. Then, answer the questions.

The Field Museum

The Field Museum is a famous museum in Chicago, Illinois. It contains exhibits of animals, plants, and people from around the world. The museum was built in 1893. It was first called the Columbian Museum of Chicago because it contained the objects for the World's Columbian Exposition of that year. Its name was changed in 1905 to honor Marshall Field, who was an early supporter. The Field Museum contains the skeleton of "Sue," the world's largest and most famous *Tyrannosaurus rex*. Visitors can find out what Sue ate and how she lived. The buildings around the museum include the Shedd Aquarium, which has marine life from tiny sea horses to large sharks, and the Adler Planetarium, where people can find out information about stars and planets. Museum workers conduct research on not only how animals have lived in the past, but how we can save endangered species today. People who visit the museum enjoy seeing the exhibits, but they also like finding out how they can help.

1. What is the main idea of this story?
   a. People like visiting the Field Museum.
   b. The Columbian Museum of Chicago was built in 1893.
   (c.) The Field Museum has exhibits on many animals, plants, and people.

2. Why was the name of the museum changed?
   to honor an early supporter named Marshall Field

3. Who is "Sue"?
   the world's largest and most famous *Tyrannosaurus rex*

4. What can you see at the Shedd Aquarium?
   marine life

5. What can you find out at the Adler Planetarium?
   information about stars and planets

6. What are some things that museum workers do?
   conduct research on how animals have lived in the past and how we can save endangered species today

CD-104306 • © Carson-Dellosa

Name _____

Read the story. Then, answer the questions.

City Services

Cities provide many services to people who live there. The mayor and city council, who are elected by the citizens of that city, make the laws that everyone must follow. They also meet to discuss community issues, such as whether to build a new recreation center. Other city employees include police officers and firefighters. These people work to keep everyone in the city safe. Other city services are at the library, where the public can check out books, and at companies that provide water and electricity. Some cities have special programs for the people who live there, such as reading clubs at the library or computer classes for senior citizens. It takes many services to make a city work. Some people like to give back to their community by doing volunteer work. They might teach swimming lessons or offer to pick up litter in the parks. When everyone in a city works together, it can be a great place to live.

1. What is the main idea of this story?
   a. People living in a city receive many services.
   b. Some people like to give back to their community.
   c. A library is a place where people can check out books.

2. Who elects the mayor and city council?
   the citizens who live in a city

3. What do the mayor and city council members do?
   make city laws and meet to discuss community issues

4. Name three employees who work for the city.
   Answers may vary.

5. What kinds of programs might a city have?
   Answers may vary.

6. How can people help their community?
   Answers may vary.

76   CD-104306 • © Carson-Dellosa

Name _____

Read the story. Then, answer the questions.

Family Trees

Have you ever heard of a family tree? A family tree is not a plant that grows in the park. It is a drawing that shows how everyone in your family is related. The branches of the tree show different parts of your family. Before you begin to create a family tree, you should find out the names of as many family members as you can. Research this by asking your relatives. Then, begin to draw your tree. Write your name in the middle. Next to your name, write the names of your siblings. Above your name, write the names of your parents or stepparents. Above each of their names, write the names of their parents. You may want to draw a picture of each person or use photographs. Building the tree together can be a fun activity for the whole family. You may find out you are related to someone famous!

1. What is the main idea of this story?
   a. A family tree is not a plant that grows in the park.
   b. A family tree shows how everyone in your family is related.
   c. You may want to draw pictures on the family tree.

2. What do the branches of a family tree show?
   different parts of your family

3. Why should you talk to relatives about the family tree?
   because they will know names of people that you may not know

4. Where do you write your name on a family tree?
   in the middle

5. What goes above each name on a family tree?
   that person's parents or stepparents

6. What might you discover as you make your family tree?
   Answers may vary.

CD-104306 • © Carson-Dellosa   77

Name _____

Read the story. Then, answer the questions.

Reading Maps

Have you ever used a map to plan a route? A world map shows the outlines of the continents and seas. It may have parts shaded brown and green to show areas of desert or forest. A city map shows important buildings such as the library or city hall, as well as city streets. Maps use symbols to help you understand them. A compass rose looks like an eight-pointed star inside a circle. It shows you the directions north, south, east, and west. North is usually at the top. A map scale tells you how distances on the map relate to the real world. For example, one inch (2.5 cm) on the map may be equal to 100 miles (160.9 km). A map legend shows you what other symbols mean. A black dot may stand for a city, a star inside a circle may mean a country's capital city, and an airplane may be used to represent an airport. Knowing what these symbols mean makes it much easier to travel.

1. What is the main idea of this story?
   a. Some maps use a compass rose and a scale.
   b. A world map is very different from a city map.
   c. Maps use symbols to help you understand them.

2. What does a world map show you?
   continents, seas, areas of desert and forest

3. What does a city map show you?
   city buildings and streets

4. Why do you use a compass rose?
   to tell the directions on a map

5. What does a map scale tell you?
   how distances on the map relate to the real world

6. List some symbols used on a map.
   Answers may vary.

78   CD-104306 • © Carson-Dellosa

Name _____

Read the story. Then, answer the questions.

Latitude and Longitude

Latitude and longitude are ways of dividing Earth into regions. Latitude lines run around the globe from east to west. The line around the middle is called the equator. Latitude is measured using the equator as zero. The lines around Earth as you move north are labeled with positive numbers. The lines going south are negative. Longitude lines run north to south from the north pole to the south pole. The zero point, called the Prime Meridian, for longitude is the line that runs through Greenwich, England. Positive values go east, and negative values go west. Both measurements are given in degrees. The latitude of Ottawa, the capital of Canada, is 45° 25' 0" N, which is read as "forty-five degrees, twenty-five minutes, zero seconds north." Latitude and longitude have long been used by people who study geography and map-making, as well as by explorers who travel around the globe. With the invention of the GPS, or global positioning system, many more people can find their exact location on Earth.

1. What is the main idea of this story?
   a. Latitude and longitude tell your exact location on Earth.
   b. Longitude is measured in degrees.
   c. The latitude of Ottawa is 45° 25' 0" N.

2. What is the line around the middle of Earth called?
   the equator

3. Which places on Earth do longitude lines start and end at?
   the north and south poles

4. Where is the zero point for longitude?
   Greenwich, England

5. Which people might use latitude and longitude most often?
   people who study geography and map-making; explorers who travel around the globe

6. Why might people want to know their exact location on Earth?
   Answers may vary.

CD-104306 • © Carson-Dellosa   79

Worksheet 1 (page 80)

Name _____

Cloze

Nouns

A noun is a word that names a person, place, or thing. Read the story below. Some of the nouns are missing. Fill in the blanks with the words from the word box below.

bunch	dessert	table	grandmother	garden
backyard	cookbooks	dishes	pie	birthday
autumn	kitchen	recipes	flowers	house

Margie liked to visit her **grandmother** after school. Grandmother's **house** was full of fun things to explore. In the **backyard** was a beautiful **garden** with sweet-smelling **flowers** . Margie had helped Grandmother plant them last **autumn** . Grandmother's large **kitchen** had old **cookbooks** to read through. They were filled with **recipes** for yummy **dishes** . Margie's favorite **dessert** was strawberry **pie** . She hoped Grandmother would make one for her **birthday** . Margie would offer to help! She would pick a **bunch** of flowers for the dining room **table** .

80   CD-104306 • © Carson-Dellosa

Worksheet 2 (page 81)

Name _____

Cloze

Nouns

A noun is a word that names a person, place, or thing. Read the story below. Some of the nouns are missing. Fill in the blanks with the words from the word box below.

apartment	brother	students	art	family
library	place	state	teacher	notice
school	work	mother	club	projects

Raven and her little **brother** needed a new **place** to go after school. They usually went to their aunt's **apartment** , but she was moving to another **state** . Raven's **mother** did not finish **work** early enough to pick them up at school. Raven saw a **notice** at **school** about a new **club** that was forming. It was for **students** aged eight to ten. They would meet after school, walk to the **library** with the art **teacher** , and work on art **projects** until someone from their **family** could come get them. Raven thought that was perfect! She loved **art** , and so did her brother. She could not wait to tell Mom.

81   CD-104306 • © Carson-Dellosa

Worksheet 3 (page 82)

Name _____

Cloze

Nouns

A noun is a word that names a person, place, or thing. Read the story below. Some of the nouns are missing. Fill in the blanks with the words from the word box below.

family	suit	hills	weekend	dad
neighborhood	park	socks	sister	store
hobby	morning	lunchtime	block	shoes

Lakshmi's **dad** loved to run. He ran down the streets in their **neighborhood** every **morning** before sunrise. Then, he ran once around the **block** at **lunchtime** . He also ran up and down the steep **hills** by the city **park** each **weekend** morning. Lakshmi thought this **hobby** looked like fun. She asked her dad if she could run with him. Dad said, "Sure!" He took Lakshmi to the **store** to buy a track **suit** and **socks** that would keep her feet dry. Finally, they bought running **shoes** . Now Lakshmi's older **sister** wants to run too! Soon, her whole **family** will be running.

82   CD-104306 • © Carson-Dellosa

Worksheet 4 (page 83)

Name _____

Cloze

Nouns

A noun is a word that names a person, place, or thing. Read the story below. Some of the nouns are missing. Fill in the blanks with the words from the word box below.

topic	something	class	model	magnets
salad	ideas	planets	system	tomatoes
advice	stepdad	project	plants	garden

Stefani needed to choose a creative **project** for science **class** . First, she wanted to study **magnets** . She could show how to pull them apart. Then, she thought she would build a **model** of the solar **system** . She could show how the different **planets** moved. Finally, Stefani thought about growing tomato **plants** . She liked working in the **garden** . Stefani had many good **ideas** . She asked her **stepdad** which **topic** to choose. He said, "Pick **something** that the whole family will enjoy." Stefani thought that was great **advice** . She decided to grow **tomatoes** . She could make a tasty **salad** when she was done!

83   CD-104306 • © Carson-Dellosa

Page 84

Name _____

Verbs

A verb is a word that tells what kind of action is being performed. Read the story below. Some of the verbs are missing. Fill in the blanks with the words from the word box below.

hopes	practice	kicks	knows	move
quizzes	score	rides	runs	is
says	join	learn	tries	loves

Jamie **loves** to be active. He **rides** his bike after school, and he **runs** with his mom on weekends. He **hopes** to **join** the soccer team next year. His sister, Kim, has been helping him **practice** . She **is** the goalie for the high school team. Jamie always **kicks** the ball straight into the net when he plays with his sister. Kim **says** Jamie must **learn** all the rules before he **tries** out for the team. She **quizzes** him on how to **score** a goal and when to **move** up the field. Kim **knows** that Jamie will be a great addition to the team!

84   CD-104306 • © Carson-Dellosa

Page 85

Name _____

Verbs

A verb is a word that tells what kind of action is being performed. Read the story below. Some of the verbs are missing. Fill in the blanks with the words from the word box below.

fry	like	picks	tastes	stop
arrive	buy	helps	wait	take
have	wake	brings	puts	cast

Benny and his sister Hannah **like** to go fishing with their uncle. They **wake** up early on a Saturday morning. Uncle Ray **picks** them up in his old pickup truck. He **brings** fishing rods and an icebox. They **stop** to **buy** bait and cold drinks on the way to the lake. When they **arrive** , Uncle Ray **puts** the bait on the hook. He **helps** Benny and Hannah **cast** their lines into the water. Then, they **wait** for a fish to **take** the bait. Soon they **have** enough fish for dinner. They **fry** the fish with vegetables. It **tastes** great!

CD-104306 • © Carson-Dellosa   85

Page 86

Name _____

Verbs

A verb is a word that tells what kind of action is being performed. Read the story below. Some of the verbs are missing. Fill in the blanks with the words from the word box below.

laugh	watch	showed	dressed	sounded
went	were	felt	looked	smiled
play	loved	called	cheered	was

Keesha **loved** to **watch** her older sister, Kendra, **play** volleyball. She **dressed** in the colors for Kendra's school and **went** to all of the games. She **cheered** until she **sounded** hoarse. Kendra **called** Keesha her biggest fan. Keesha **felt** sad that she **was** too small to play volleyball. Kendra and the rest of her teammates **were** very tall. One day Keesha's mom **showed** her a picture of Kendra when she was Keesha's age. Kendra **looked** just like Keesha did now. Keesha **smiled** and started to **laugh** . "Kendra was small once too! Maybe I can play volleyball one day after all."

86   CD-104306 • © Carson-Dellosa

Page 87

Name _____

Verbs

A verb is a word that tells what kind of action is being performed. Read the story below. Some of the verbs are missing. Fill in the blanks with the words from the word box below.

gets	called	has	walked	loves
started	come	exercise	stepped	would
does	walks	trusts	works	opened

Kamran **has** a new afterschool job. His neighbor, Mr. Quigley, just **started** coaching soccer in the evenings, and he **does** not have time to **come** home after work. Mr. Quigley said he **trusts** Kamran to **exercise** his dog, Leo. Kamran **walks** Leo to the park and back before he **works** on his homework. On the first day of Kamran's new job, he **opened** the gate and **called** Leo's name. Leo came running. He was ready for his walk! As Kamran and Leo **walked** down the street, another neighbor, Mrs. Pellini, **stepped** out of her house. She asked, "Kamran, **would** you walk my dog too? Katie **loves** to go to the park." Now Kamran **gets** twice the exercise!

CD-104306 • © Carson-Dellosa   87

Page 88

Name _____

Cloze

Adjectives

An adjective is a word that describes something. Read the story below. Some of the adjectives are missing. Fill in the blanks with the words from the word box below.

enormous	beautiful	dark	quiet	awful
better	great	inspiring	fine	sad
nervous	cheerful	deep	bright	shaky

My choir director, Mrs. Rosas, is an **inspiring** person. She helps us memorize **beautiful** songs so that we can give a **fine** performance. When I tried out for the choir, I was very **nervous**. My voice was **quiet** and **shaky**, and I thought that I sounded **awful**. Mrs. Rosas smiled and said she knew that I could do a **better** job. She told me to take a **deep** breath and try the song again. This time I sounded **great**! Our choir wears **bright** red shirts with **dark** pants when we sing. Being in the choir makes me feel **cheerful**. If I am **sad** when I start singing, by the end of the song I have an **enormous** smile on my face again.

Page 89

Name _____

Cloze

Adjectives

An adjective is a word that describes something. Read the story below. Some of the adjectives are missing. Fill in the blanks with the words from the word box below.

marvelous	wonderful	older	fun	favorite
lengthy	yellow	giant	blue	nice
closest	fabulous	special	front	long

Order of some adjectives may vary.

Leticia and her **older** brother, Amos, wanted to plan a **wonderful** surprise party for their mom. She always threw parties for them that were **fabulous** and **fun**. Now it would be her own **special** day. Leticia made a **long** list of all of her mom's **closest** friends. Mom was such a **nice** person, everyone wanted to be her friend. Amos ordered a **giant** cake with **blue** and **yellow** icing to feed all of the guests. These were Mom's **favorite** colors. On the day of the party, Leticia asked Mom to go on a **lengthy** walk. When they got home, all of Mom's friends were hiding in the living room. When Mom opened the **front** door, they all shouted, "Surprise!" Mom said it was the most **marvelous** party ever.

Page 90

Name _____

Cloze

Adjectives

An adjective is a word that describes something. Read the story below. Some of the adjectives are missing. Fill in the blanks with the words from the word box below.

famous	long	vast	slender	longer
brilliant	creative	green	deep	tall
dark	tiny	best	whole	great

Order of some adjectives may vary.

Angelica decided to write a book. She loved to read, and her teachers said that she had a **great** imagination. Her heroine would have **green** eyes and **long** **dark** hair, just like Angelica. She would live in the middle of a **vast** **deep** forest. Angelica imagined the animals that might come to visit her character— **tall** bears, **slender** deer, and **tiny** mice. She worked on her story every day at lunchtime and after school. It grew **longer** and soon took up a **whole** notebook! Angelica let her **best** friend, Mindy, read her story. Mindy thought it was **brilliant** and very **creative**. She said she could not wait until Angelica was a **famous** author one day!

Page 91

Name _____

Cloze

Adjectives

An adjective is a word that describes something. Read the story below. Some of the adjectives are missing. Fill in the blanks with the words from the word box below.

perfect	little	new	older	cute
thick	wide	bright	strong	old
entire	sturdy	soft	baby	yellow

Order of some adjectives may vary.

Marcel's dad wanted to buy a **new** truck. His **old** one had too **little** space for the **entire** family to be comfortable. Marcel's mom wanted something with **soft** seats and room for his **baby** sister's car seat and her **cute** dolls. Marcel's **older** brother wanted something **sturdy** enough to go camping in. Marcel thought it would be fun to have a **bright** yellow truck. His friends would love it! One day, Marcel's dad came home in a new **yellow** truck. It had **wide**, **thick** seats, and it was **strong** enough to go camping! Marcel thought it was the **perfect** truck for their family.

Name _____

Missing Words

Read the story below. Every tenth word is missing. Fill in the blanks with the words from the word box below.

the	did	They	needed
her	glad	Saturday	elderly
Amber	make	what	were

Amber belonged to a special club that met every **Saturday**. The club was not a sports team. The members **did** not play board games. It was a community club. **Amber** and her friends worked to make their neighborhood better. **They** made sure the sidewalks were clear and people's driveways **were** clean. They held yard sales to raise money to **make** new signs for the park so that people would know **what** time it closed. Amber's favorite project was helping the **elderly**. She liked to help her grandmother, and many of **her** grandmother's friends lived in the same neighborhood. Sometimes they **needed** their flowers watered or asked for help walking to **the** store. Helping others made Amber feel good. She was **glad** she had joined the club!

CD-104306 • © Carson-Dellosa

Name _____

Missing Words

Read the story below. Every tenth word is missing. Fill in the blanks with the words from the word box below.

gave	the	her	school
Bella	felt	along	their
out	Mabel	to	school

Bella and her classmates had been practicing for the **school** play for weeks. Bella was playing the queen, and **her** friend Gerry was the king. They had made crowns **out** of aluminum foil. Stacey and Aaron painted the posters **to** show the forest scene behind them. They would perform **their** play for all of the younger students at their **school**. Bella's little sister, Mabel, had been helping her rehearse. **Bella** hoped Mabel would not try to say the lines **along** with her! On the day of the play, Bella **felt** nervous. She peeked out into the crowd and saw **Mabel** sitting with her friends. Mabel waved at her and **gave** her a smile. Bella began to relax. She knew **the** students would love the play.

CD-104306 • © Carson-Dellosa

Name _____

Missing Words

Read the story below. Every eighth word is missing. Fill in the blanks with the words from the word box below.

He	let	play	giggle
small	dog	back	the
Warren	him		Warren

Warren loved his new little puppy, Jojo. **He** had white fur and big brown eyes. **Warren** ran home from school every day to **let** Jojo out and play with him in **the** backyard. Jojo was always glad to see **him**. Jojo licked Warren's hand and made him **giggle**. Warren hoped he could teach Jojo to **play** fetch. His friend Vicky had a bigger **dog** named Lucky. Lucky knew how to bring **back** sticks and tennis balls. Jojo was too **small** to carry a tennis ball now, but **Warren** knew he would grow bigger one day.

CD-104306 • © Carson-Dellosa

Name _____

Missing Words

Read the story below. Every eighth word is missing. Fill in the blanks with the words from the word box below.

keep	the	work	test
for	picnic	last	studied
news	the	to	proud

Julio had a wonderful surprise at school **last** week. He made the highest grade in **the** class on his math test! Julio had **studied** hard for a whole week before the **test**. He asked his stepmom to check over **the** problems he worked for practice. His hard **work** paid off! Julio ran home after school **to** tell his dad and stepmom the good **news**. They hugged him and said they were **proud** of him. They planned a special treat **for** the weekend. They went on a family **picnic** to the park. Julio thought he would **keep** working hard to do well in math.

CD-104306 • © Carson-Dellosa

Page 96

Name _____ **Cloze**

Missing Words

Read the story below. Every fifth word is missing. Fill in the blanks with the words from the word box below.

their	Trudy	lived	dad
town	same	cousin	knew
Trudy	be	kept	good
and	family	had	but

Heidi and her cousin **Trudy** were best friends. They **lived** in different towns but **kept** in touch by e-mail **and** telephone. One day Heidi's **dad** said he had some **good** news for her. Trudy's **family** was moving to their **town**! Heidi was excited. She **had** good friends at school, **but** they were not the **same** as having her own **cousin** in her class. She **knew** her friends would like **Trudy** too. And she would **be** a great addition to **their** soccer team!

Page 97

Name _____ **Cloze**

Missing Words

Read the story below. Every fifth word is missing. Fill in the blanks with the words from the word box below.

music	move	When	instrument
plays	Zak's	Now	is
a	his	him	it
Learning	claps	play	for

Zak is learning to **play** the violin. His stepdad **is** teaching him how to **move** the bow and place **his** fingers on the strings. **When** Zak first started playing, **it** sounded like fingernails on **a** chalkboard. His stepdad told **him** not to give up. **Learning** to play a musical **instrument** takes time and patience. **Now** Zak can play melodies **for** his family. His stepdad **plays** along on the guitar. **Zak's** little sister smiles and **claps** her hands to the **music**.

Page 98

Name _____ **Point of View**

Point of View

Point of view refers to the person who is telling the story or "speaking." When you write a letter, you are writing in "first person," which includes the words *I, me, my, we,* and *our.* Second-person writing occurs when the author talks about *you* and *yours,* and third person includes the words *he, she, they, his, her,* and *their.* In third-person writing, the author does not put himself in the story.

A story can be told from different points of view.
In **first person**, the main character tells the story.
In **second person**, the story is told as though it is happening to you.
In **third person**, a narrator tells the story as if she is watching it happen.

Read each story and circle the point of view.

Marcus's family had just moved to a large city from a very small town. He was surprised at how many cars were on the street and how few people said hello when he met them on the sidewalk. In his old town, he had known everyone. He hoped that he would make a new friend on the first day of school. When he saw the crowded hallways as he walked into the building, he felt worried. Then, he thought to himself that with all those people around, he was sure to make a lot of friends.

First Person   Second Person   (Third Person)

When my family moved to the big city, I was excited about all of the new activities we could try. I never thought about how crowded it might be. Back home, my neighbors were very friendly. It seemed like I knew everyone in the whole town. I wanted to make new friends in the city, but when I got to school the hallways were so packed I could hardly get to my classroom. I took a deep breath and thought to myself, "With all of these people around, I am sure to make new friends."

(First Person)   Second Person   Third Person

You and your family have just moved to the city. You are surprised at seeing so many cars on the road. In your old town, you felt like you knew everyone. When you drive up to the school, your mother wishes you good luck. You walk into the building and start to look for your classroom. You think that with all these people around, you are sure to make some new friends.

First Person   (Second Person)   Third Person

Page 99

Name _____ **Point of View**

Point of View

Point of view refers to the person who is telling the story or "speaking." When you write a letter, you are writing in "first person," which includes the words *I, me, my, we,* and *our.* Second-person writing occurs when the author talks about *you* and *yours,* and third person includes the words *he, she, they, his, her,* and *their.* In third-person writing, the author does not put himself in the story.

A story can be told from different points of view.
In **first person**, the main character tells the story.
In **second person**, the story is told as though it is happening to you.
In **third person**, a narrator tells the story as if she is watching it happen.

Read each story and circle the point of view.

I love gardening. Seeing the little sprouts push up through the ground in early spring makes my heart sing. It can be hard to wait until the plants are fully grown to eat them. My brother likes vegetables, and he enjoys tomatoes in particular. Every year he tries to harvest them too early. At the end of the summer, I gather seeds and plant my crop for the next year. It is fun to see the whole growing cycle.

(First Person)   Second Person   Third Person

You love to work in the garden. You especially like seeing the tiny plants first appear through the dirt. Although it is hard to wait, you know that it is better to wait until the plants are fully grown before pulling them up. Your brother is so fond of tomatoes that his mouth begins to water even before they are red. At summer's end, you gather seeds to plant for next spring. You rejoice at the cycle of nature.

First Person   (Second Person)   Third Person

Carrie often worked in her garden. She checked the soil every morning to see if any new plants had appeared. Sometimes her brother tried to pick a green tomato, but she always stopped him. She said that it was better to wait until they were ripe. When the summer was over, she planted seeds for a new crop.

First Person   Second Person   (Third Person)

Name _____

Point of View

Point of view refers to the person who is telling the story or "speaking." When you write a letter, you are writing in "first person," which includes the words *I, me, my, we,* and *our.* Second-person writing occurs when the author talks about *you* and *yours,* and third person includes the words *he, she, they, his, her,* and *their.* In third-person writing, the author does not put himself in the story.

A story can be told from different points of view.
In **first person**, the main character tells the story.
In **second person**, the story is told as though it is happening to you.
In **third person**, a narrator tells the story as if she is watching it happen.

Read each story and circle the point of view.

Felipe loved to cook. He had been helping his mom and grandma in the kitchen ever since he could remember. One day Mom suggested he cook dinner for Grandma. Felipe was nervous but excited. He wrote a grocery list and asked Mom to take him shopping. They chose fresh vegetables and herbs for a delicious stew. Felipe had watched Grandma cook the stew many times. He thought he could cook it perfectly even without a recipe, as long as Mom was there to answer any questions.

First Person   Second Person   (Third Person)

I love to cook. I first started helping my mom and grandma in the kitchen when I was very small. One day Mom suggested I cook dinner for Grandma. I felt excited but also a little nervous. I had never cooked a meal by myself before! Mom and I went to the store with a list of food to buy. She showed me how to choose fresh vegetables and special herbs. I have watched Grandma make stew many times, so I think that I can cook it even without a list of instructions. Mom will be standing by to help just in case.

(First Person)   Second Person   Third Person

Your favorite activity is cooking. You have been helping your family in the kitchen since you were a child. One day your mom suggests you cook dinner for Grandma. You are excited but nervous, since you have never cooked a whole dinner by yourself before. You help your mom make a list of things to buy, and then you go to the store. You pick out only the freshest vegetables. Because you have watched Grandma make her special stew many times before, you know you can make it without using a recipe and with only a little help from Mom.

First Person   (Second Person)   Third Person

     CD-104306 • © Carson-Dellosa

Name _____

Point of View

Point of view refers to the person who is telling the story or "speaking." When you write a letter, you are writing in "first person," which includes the words *I, me, my, we,* and *our.* Second-person writing occurs when the author talks about *you* and *yours,* and third person includes the words *he, she, they, his, her,* and *their.* In third-person writing, the author does not put himself in the story.

A story can be told from different points of view.
In **first person**, the main character tells the story.
In **second person**, the story is told as though it is happening to you.
In **third person**, a narrator tells the story as if she is watching it happen.

Read each story and circle the point of view.

You have been looking forward to the big class picnic for a long time. You and your friends hope to look for wildflowers after you eat lunch. You want to find 10 different kinds of flowers. When the day of the picnic comes, it starts to rain. You are sad at first, but then your teacher reminds you that the flowers need rain to grow. You smile to yourself and think that next time you can try to find 20 different wildflowers.

First Person   (Second Person)   Third Person

I had been looking forward to the class picnic for weeks. My friends and I were planning to pick wildflowers after eating our sandwiches. I hoped I could find 10 different kinds of flowers! On the day of the picnic, it was raining. I felt sad at first, but I knew that the rain would help the flowers grow even bigger. The next time we went on a picnic, maybe I could find 20 kinds of flowers!

(First Person)   Second Person   Third Person

Dreama and her friends had been looking forward to the class picnic all month long. They wanted to eat sandwiches in the field and then pick beautiful wildflowers. Dreama was hoping to find 10 different kinds of flowers. When she woke up on the day of the picnic, it was raining. Dreama felt sad at first, but she knew that the flowers needed rain to grow. Maybe at the next picnic she could find even more kinds of flowers.

First Person   Second Person   (Third Person)

CD-104306 • © Carson-Dellosa

Name _____

Point of View

Point of view refers to the person who is telling the story or "speaking." When you write a letter, you are writing in "first person," which includes the words *I, me, my, we,* and *our.* Second-person writing occurs when the author talks about *you* and *yours,* and third person includes the words *he, she, they, his, her,* and *their.* In third-person writing, the author does not put himself in the story.

A story can be told from different points of view.
In **first person**, the main character tells the story.
In **second person**, the story is told as though it is happening to you.
In **third person**, a narrator tells the story as if she is watching it happen.

Read each story and circle the point of view.

Clara ran home from school and checked the mailbox. She was disappointed to find that the mail had not come yet. She was expecting a letter from a special friend. Clara had a pen pal in Korea named Chi. They sometimes sent e-mail to each other, but both girls liked getting letters and funny postcards too. Just then there was a knock at the door. It was the postman! He smiled and handed Clara a letter with a Korean postmark.

First Person   Second Person   (Third Person)

I ran home from school yesterday and checked the mailbox. My letter from Chi was not there yet! Chi is my pen pal. She lives in Korea. We sometimes send e-mail to each other, but we both like getting postcards with funny pictures too. I was getting a snack when I heard a knock at the door. It was the mailman, and he had a letter for me! He smiled and said, "Tell Chi I said hello."

(First Person)   Second Person   Third Person

You run home from school to check the mailbox. You are disappointed when the letter you are expecting is not there. You are hoping for a letter from your pen pal, Chi, who lives in Korea. You like to send e-mail to each other, but you also like getting postcards and letters in the mail. You hear a knock at the door. It is the mailman, and he has a letter from Chi.

First Person   (Second Person)   Third Person

     CD-104306 • © Carson-Dellosa

Name _____

Point of View

Point of view refers to the person who is telling the story or "speaking." When you write a letter, you are writing in "first person," which includes the words *I, me, my, we,* and *our.* Second-person writing occurs when the author talks about *you* and *yours,* and third person includes the words *he, she, they, his, her,* and *their.* In third-person writing, the author does not put himself in the story.

A story can be told from different points of view.
In **first person**, the main character tells the story.
In **second person**, the story is told as though it is happening to you.
In **third person**, a narrator tells the story as if she is watching it happen.

Read each story and circle the point of view.

I like rain, and I like sun, but I like snow most of all. Winter is a fun season. I like building snowmen with my brothers and making a fort with snowballs. I like lying in the snow and making patterns with my arms. I help Dad shovel snow off the pathways so that people can walk and drive safely. I also help Mom make cocoa and cookies to warm us up when we come back indoors.

(First Person)   Second Person   Third Person

Lupe liked all kinds of weather, but she liked snow most of all. Winter was her favorite season. She liked to build snowmen with her brothers. Sometimes they made a fort with snowballs. Lupe liked to lie in the snow and make patterns with her arms. She helped her dad shovel the sidewalks so that people could walk safely. She also helped her mom make cocoa and bake cookies to warm everyone up when they came back indoors.

First Person   Second Person   (Third Person)

You like rain and sun, but you like the snow in winter most of all. You like to build snowmen with your brothers and make forts with snowballs. You like to lie in the snow and make patterns with your arms. You help your father move snow off the sidewalks. Then, you help your mom make cocoa and cookies to warm everyone up!

First Person   (Second Person)   Third Person

CD-104306 • © Carson-Dellosa

Congratulations!

_____

_____

receives this award for

_____

Signed _____

Date _____

adapt

anchor

behavior

carnation

admit

assist

blizzard

celebrate

affect

atmosphere

brilliant

climate

ambition

background

candidate

colonial

compete	concrete	deserve	detective
© CD	© CD	© CD	© CD

district	earnest	economy	electron
© CD	© CD	© CD	© CD

encounter	enormous	exchange	forecast
© CD	© CD	© CD	© CD

fossil	frequent	garment	gesture
© CD	© CD	© CD	© CD

glimpse	goal	harvest	hesitate
© CD	© CD	© CD	© CD
identify	intelligence	intestines	latitude
© CD	© CD	© CD	© CD
longitude	magnificent	maintain	marvelous
© CD	© CD	© CD	© CD
mingle	museum	nucleus	numerous
© CD	© CD	© CD	© CD

outcome

© CD

patient

© CD

protect

© CD

rejoice

© CD

organize

© CD

particular

© CD

preserve

© CD

recover

© CD

organism

© CD

overlook

© CD

plot

© CD

publish

© CD

orbit

© CD

outline

© CD

peculiar

© CD

propose

© CD

reveal	seldom	slight	temperature
repair	scarce	signal	suspend
renew	route	shift	stagger
remark	rotate	shield	sole

thorough	transmit	trial	underground
universal	vaccination	valuable	vessel
victory	violin	visible	volcano
voyage	weave	wilderness	yield

© CD